Curriculum Connections for
Tree House Travelers for Grades K-4

Jane Berner, Sabrina Minser, and Helen Burkart Presser

Linworth
Books

Professional Development Resources for K–12
Library Media and Technology Specialists

Berner, Jane.
  Curriculum connections for tree house travelers for grades K-4 / Jane Berner, Sabrina
Minser, and Helen Burkart Presser.
      p. cm.
  Includes bibliographical references and index.
  ISBN 1-58683-281-6 (pbk.)
  1. Education, Elementary--Curricula. 2. Education, Elementary--Activity programs.
3. Interdisciplinary approach in education. 4. Elementary school teaching. I. Minser,
Sabrina. II. Presser, Helen Burkart. III. Title.
  LB1570.B44 2007
  372.19--dc22
                              2007015407

Cynthia Anderson: Acquisitions Editor
Carol Simpson: Editorial Director
Judi Repman: Consulting Editor

Published by Linworth Publishing, Inc.
3650 Olentangy River Road, Suite 250
Columbus, Ohio 43214

ISBN: 1-58683-281-6

5 4 3 2 1

About the Authors

 Jane Berner has taught 11 years at a private elementary school, drawing attention to her creative implementation of art and the study of artists throughout the curriculum. Berner has a bachelor's degree in general studies with a major in fine arts and psychology. Her love of literature and the benefit that it brings to the classroom has led Jane to build her curriculum around quality books. Book illustrations inspire Ms. Berner to create diverse multidisciplinary projects that make her classroom an exciting place for children. She has been a guest speaker in school, college, and library conference settings. Berner currently teaches Kindergarten Prep at Canterbury School.

 Sabrina Minser is an innovative computer teacher who has taught in private elementary schools for more than 15 years. In addition to basic technology skills, her curriculum brings books and technology together. Ms. Minser's background as a computer specialist has enabled her to train teachers to use technology to enhance their existing curriculum. She is a member of Indiana Computer Educators, and is currently the Lower School technology specialist at Canterbury School.

Helen Burkart Presser is an award-winning teacher and librarian who has implemented two school libraries and has taught in both public and private school settings for over 28 years. In addition to  teaching literature and reference skills to elementary students, she has taught children's literature classes at the university level. Presser spent years reviewing books for her columns in LIBRARY TALK magazine, and has published numerous articles. She holds a bachelor's degree in elementary education and a master's degree in library science. Presser studied the art of writing for children under Caldecott medalist, Uri Shulevitz, and she recently received a grant to travel to Germany to follow in the footsteps of the Brothers Grimm. A member of the Society of Children's Book Writers and Illustrators, she is currently Lower School librarian at Canterbury School.

Acknowledgments

Special thanks to each of our families for their love, encouragement, and support; our colleagues and friends at Canterbury School for their creative inspiration; and the Children's Librarians of Allen County Public Library for their assistance in helping us procure extensive collections of books.

Table of Contents

Table of Figures

Introduction and Purpose

Curriculum Connections for Tree House Travelers for Grades K-4 is a literature-based resource guide for library media specialists, primary and intermediate level teachers, and elementary education students. The purpose of this book is to offer a workable model of an in-depth study of time and place. Students travel to high interest destinations, experiencing each place through quality literature, foods, multimedia, and cross-curricular activities that incorporate differentiated learning and Bloom's Taxonomy.

The idea for this book had its roots in a literature-based summer school program for primary grade level children, taught as a collaborative effort between librarian, technology specialist, and classroom teacher.

Destinations follow the sequence of the first four books of the Magic Tree House series. Each unit is launched by one of the Magic Tree House books and its research companion, setting the stage for an in-depth study of the topic. The series serves to connect the four units as well as provide primary grade students with a high interest, easy reading chapter book series. Quality literature, media, and Web sites are a natural extension.

How to Use This Book

Each unit is laid out in the same format, including a Unit Passport, Travel Itinerary, Classroom Setting, Supplies and Word Wall, Magic Tree House Book Annotations and Connections, Book Web and corresponding Curriculum Web, Supporting Unit Curriculum Connections, Art Arena, Theme Cuisine, and Culminating Activities. Multimedia Resource, Web Site Resource, and Book Resource sections follow the activities in each unit. Activity worksheets and project templates are located at the end of each unit.

Media specialists and teachers begin each unit by requesting a school or public library book collection, using the single page Book Web. The corresponding Curriculum Web aids in selecting unit activities. To help plan a day, week, or month long unit, use the *Model for Unit Study* template, figure 0.10 on page xiii. Each unit includes a Station Rotations plan, to allow for differentiated learning and an assessment rubric. On page xvii see figure 0.8, *Cross-Curricular Activities Chart*, to aid in pairing activities with state or national standards.

Model For Unit Study

Day 1	Day 2	Day 3	Day 4	Day 5
Dinosaurs Before Dark *Dinosaurs Research Guide #1* *Dinosaur books* **Introductory Activities**	**Introductory Activities**	**Developmental Activities**	**Developmental Activities**	**Culminating Activities**
Library: Introduce unit: book talk dinosaur related books Introductory, hands-on activity	**Library:** Continue introductory activities Reading time in reading corner, conduct book chats	**Library:** Create your own dinostore prop for the poetry break	**Library:** Practice a poetry break –*(Dinostore)*	**Library:** Perform a poetry break for your guests *(Dinostore)*
Computer Time: Visit some dinosaur Web sites	**Computer Time:** Complete one of the computer projects. Ex. Dinosaur Internet Scavenger Hunt	**Computer Time:** Create Name-a-saurus with a computer drawing program	**Computer Time:** Discuss Internet safety and complete one of the Internet research projects	**Computer Time:** Journal a day in the life of a dinosaur using a word processing program
Classroom Time: Classroom Setting, Word wall Dinosaur math activity Dinosaur language arts activity Dinosaur art activity	**Classroom Time:** Dinosaur math activity Dinosaur science activity Watch *Patrick's Dinosaur* video	**Classroom Time:** Dinosaur math activity Dinosaur science activity Dinosaur art activity	**Classroom Time:** Dinosaur social studies activity (dinosaur timeline) Dinosaur *Art Arena* activity: Van Gogh style painting	**Classroom Time:** Invite another class or parents to your "Dinosaur Museum" Serve *Dinosaur Dirt Dig Pudding* or *Dinosaur Bones*, display projects and activities completed during the unit
Supplies for the day: Classroom setting supplies Activity supplies Various topic related books	**Supplies for the day:** Activity supplies	**Supplies for the day:** Activity supplies: *(Dinostore)* Cardboard boxes, paint paper, plastic dinosaurs, etc.	**Supplies for the day:** Activity supplies	**Supplies for the day:** Recipe ingredients, cups, napkins, etc.

Figure 0.10 Model for Unit Study

Book Cover Acknowledgments

Introductory Letter to Teachers and Librarians

Dear teachers and librarians,

We invite you to travel with us on an exciting trip. We hope you and your class will join us as we visit the world of dinosaurs, knights, mummies, and pirates. Tree House Travelers enjoy quality literature and cross-curricular activities as they take a trip to each destination. Students read books, prepare foods, and create projects developed for each topic.

We use Magic Tree House books to set the stage. This high interest series is just right for getting children excited about the subject area and offers primary grade students a series of books for independent reading. Each unit is introduced by reading excerpts from the unit featured Magic Tree House book and research guide, followed by extension activities. Book chats follow on a regular basis led by students who complete a book from the unit. More formal discussions take place in literature circles, where students are grouped according to the book they are reading.

Time travelers further explore subject matter through an extensive selection of quality literature, multimedia materials, multidisciplinary projects, and related Web sites. This guide is intended to be a useful resource as you, and your class, accompany us on our journey to these exciting destinations. Thanks for joining us.

Your tour guides,
Jane Berner
Sabrina Minser
Helen Burkart Presser

Cross-Curricular Activities Chart

		Unit 1 Dinosaurs	Unit 2 Medieval Times	Unit 3 Ancient Egypt	Unit 4 Pirates
Music	Vocal		27		5
	Instruments		11	10	4
Theater		7, 8, 11, 17	6, 21	8	2, 7, 14, 15
Language Arts	Reading	7, 8, 11, 17, 18, 19	19, 23, 25, 26, 32, 35, 36	11, 16, 17, 18, 19	7, 10, 12, 13, 14, 17, 19, 30
	Writing	12, 13, 15, 16, 17, 18, 19, 32, 34	19, 21, 23, 26, 28, 29, 30, 33, 34, 35, 46	11, 15, 16, 17, 18, 19, 35, 36, 38, 39	9, 12, 15, 16, 17, 18, 20, 23, 24, 37, 38, 39, 49
	Speaking	7, 8, 9, 10, 19, 25,	21, 26, 44	8, 12, 18, 19, 20, 21, 30, 37	11, 13
	Listening	19	36	10, 19, 20, 21	4, 11
Science	Science inquiry	1, 5, 24, 25, 27, 29	40	24, 27	28, 33
	Life Science	2, 12, 26, 28			33, 34
	Earth Science	20		28	
	Physical Science			25, 26	28, 29, 31
	Science History	41		27	
Social Studies	History	30, 33, 36	15, 20, 22, 23, 30, 33, 35, 43, 44, 45, 46, 47, 48, 49, 50, 51, 52, 53	7, 12, 13, 29, 30, 31, 32, 33, 34, 35, 39	30, 38, 39, 40, 43, 45, 47, 49, 50
	Geography	36, 40	48	36, 37	26, 27, 29, 35, 42, 46, 47, 48
Mathematics	Measurement	21, 22, 23	37, 39	29	26, 27
	Computation			22	25
	Patterns		38	3, 23	
Technology	Computer Exploration	29	10, 31		
	Research	5, 14, 20, 24, 28, 30, 31, 34, 38, 39	3, 8, 13, 16, 19, 24, 26, 27, 33, 35, 41, 42, 49, 53	39	8, 13, 27, 32, 33, 35, 36, 41, 49
	Multimedia	4	10, 24, 28, 31, 34	18	37
Fine Arts	Creating	1, 2, 3, 5, 6, 8, 9, 12, 27	1, 2, 3, 4, 5, 6, 7, 8, 9, 12, 13, 14, 15, 16, 17, 18, 50, 53	1, 2, 3, 4, 5, 6, 7, 9, 13, 14, 23, 31, 33, 39	1, 3, 6, 9, 18, 31, 34, 41
	Critiquing			39	17
	History		2, 4, 8, 38, 53	1, 14, 31	
Social Skills		9, 19, 35, 37, 42	26, 32, 44, 45, 51, 52	29, 38	21, 22, 24, 40, 44, 51

Figure 0.8 Cross-Curricular Activities Chart

From *Curriculum Connections for Tree House Travelers for Grades K-4* by Jane Berner, Sabrina Minser, and Helen Burkart Presser. Columbus, OH: Linworth Publishing, Inc. Further reproduction prohibited. Copyright © 2008.

Travel Destinations

UNIT 1

Destination: Dinosaurs

Two young explorers, Jack and Annie, travel in time to the days of dinosaurs. Students are introduced to dinosaurs through *Dinosaurs Before Dark* and its research guide, *Dinosaurs*, along with a selection of book-related projects. Readers are then immersed in dinosaur time through books, multimedia materials, Web sites, and cross-curricular activities.

UNIT 2

Destination: Medieval England

Fairytale Theater, medieval literature, multi-disciplinary projects, authentic food, games, and virtual castle tours transport travelers to the land of knights and castles after reading *The Knight at Dawn* and its research guide. Readers follow Jack and Annie to medieval England, where a knight escorts them to safety on a black horse. Travelers gain an in-depth understanding of the Middle Ages as they travel through the unit.

UNIT 3

Destination: Ancient Egypt

Traveling to ancient Egypt and the world of mummies is a natural extension for Magic Tree House fans after reading *Mummies in the Morning*, a story about Jack and Annie's visit to the land of pyramids, and its research guide, *Mummies and Pyramids*. Explorers read books about ancient Egypt, take virtual tours, and experience authentic foods, cultures, and art while learning about this time and place.

UNIT 4

Destination: Pirates

Days of deserted islands, pirate maps, hidden treasure, and nasty pirates are all part of the fare for travelers accompanying Jack and Annie to the world of high seas, as they read *Pirates Past Noon* and its research guide, *Pirates*. A treasure trove of pirate literature, creative treasure maps, treasure hunts, games, songs, cross-curricular activities, and software bring this experience to life.

Travel Itinerary

Classroom Setting

Classroom Setting Supplies	
card table	picks
cardboard	chisels
sheet	flashlights
hard hats	brushes
sleeping bag	model dinosaurs
shovels	dinosaur books

Word Wall	
paleontologist	fossil
geologist	evolution
extinction	prehistoric
herbivore	Cretaceous period
carnivore	Jurassic period
skeleton	Triassic period

Magic Tree House Book Annotations

Dinosaurs Before Dark

by Mary Pope Osborne. Illus. Sal Murdocca. Random House, 1992.
Eight-year-old Jack and his sister Annie discover a magic tree house that takes them back to dinosaur time. A mysterious Pteranodon rescues Jack when he finds himself caught between a meat-eating T. rex and a colony of Anatosauruses watching over their nests, who might stampede (Grades K-3).

Dinosaurs

by Will Osborne and Mary Pope Osborne. Illus. Sal Murdocca. Random House, 2000.
In this nonfiction companion to *Dinosaurs Before Dark*, Jack and Annie reveal strategies for researching dinosaurs to learn more about the fact behind the fiction. Researchers learn about fossils, dinosaur hunters, flesh-eaters, plant-eaters, sea monsters, flying creatures, and dinosaur neighbors (Grades K-3).

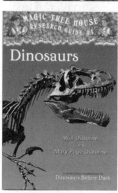

Connecting with Magic Tree House Books

Dinosaurs Before Dark Critical Thinking Questions

1. How did Jack and Annie discover the magic tree house?
2. What are Jack and Annie's interests?
3. How do you think Jack and Annie felt about landing in dinosaur time?
4. What obstacles did they overcome and how?
5. In which time period did the Pteranodon live?

Dinosaurs Before Dark Curriculum Connections

1. Design a time machine

Cover the outside classroom door with paper. Have students decorate it with dials, switches, meters, and graphs. Step through the finished machine into dinosaur time.

2. Create a pizza box suitcase

Have students decorate a pizza box to use as a suitcase as they begin their trip to the land of dinosaurs. Students create, color, and glue passport stickers to the front of the box and add a handle. Suitcases may be packed with items collected while on their dinosaur adventure unit.

3. Make a medallion

On page 31 of *Dinosaurs Before Dark*, Jack finds a gold medallion in the grass. He realizes that someone has been to the time of the dinosaurs before they arrived. Have each student form a medallion from self-hardening clay or construction paper, and then stamp an "M" on it. Paint it metallic gold. The medallion can be kept in the suitcase, along with other clues about Morgan.

4. Write a postcard

Jack and Annie write a postcard to send home, describing adventures they have encountered in dinosaur time.

Copy the *Postcard Template* figure 1.23 on cardstock (see page 32). Have students write their own dinosaur adventure postcard.

5. Make a bookmark

Have students write a book review on a bookmark, including a book summary and story elements, such as characters and setting. Students share or trade bookmarks.

6. Record your facts in a journal

A journal or index cards may be used to record facts and clues as students read about Jack and Annie's explorations. Details students unearth about the Pteranodon may also be described in their journals and housed in their pizza box suitcases. Students may check the validity of these facts using the research guide, *Dinosaurs*, and a true/false checklist.

7. Research the magnolia flower

Research the magnolia plant at: <http://en.wikipedia.org/wiki/Magnolia>. What are some products of this plant? Which state is nicknamed the "Magnolia State?" Have students draw a picture of the magnolia flower and include facts for a display.

8. Map out Jack and Annie's Magic Tree House setting

Discuss the setting of *Dinosaurs Before Dark*. Have each student draw a map of Jack and Annie's home in Frog Creek, Pennsylvania. Include the woods by the house, the magic tree house with a Pteranodon flying towards it, Frog Creek Library, the elementary school, and the park. Students may add a compass to show orientation, and a map legend.

Dinosaurs Curriculum Connections

Have students solve the following dinosaur mysteries, starting with Case #1 on page 98 of *Dinosaurs*:

1. Create an imaginary dinosaur: What colors were the dinosaurs? (Case #1: Seeing Red)

Jack and Annie's research book tells us that dinosaurs could have been colorful like today's snakes and lizards. Using

Dinosaur Fiction Books

Dinosaur Information Books

Dinosaur Book Web

Dinosaur Poetry Books

Dinosaur Art Arena Books

Dinosaur Activity Books

Fine Arts/Arts and Crafts

1. Create a Dinosaur Museum
2. Build a Pterosaur model
3. Construct a papier-mâché T. rex
4. Design a Name-a-saurus
5. Create a clay model Ankylosaurus
6. Make plaster dinosaur bones
7. Dramatize a Poetry Break
8. Create your own Dinostore and perform a poetry break
9. Design a shoebox dinobed and discuss bedtime rituals
10. Host a Hollywood Walk of Fame
11. Dramatize *All Aboard the Dinotrain*

Language Arts

12. Create a dinosaur questions flipbook
13. Create a travel guide
14. Investigate author, illustrator, Claire Ewart
15. Journal a day in the life and time of a dinosaur
16. Write a letter requesting a pet dinosaur
17. Compare *Dinorella* to *Cinderella*
18. Compare *The Dinosaur's New Clothes* to the *Emperor's New Clothes*
19. Spin a Yarn
20. Generate questions to investigate planet earth

Math

21. Calculate and compare dinosaur size differences
22. Compare size of dinosaurs to humans on a pictograph
23. Draw a dinosaur footprint to scale

Science

24. Gather information about Sue
25. Discuss how scientific discoveries have changed dinosaur fact to fiction
26. Check dinosaur facts for accuracy
27. Make your own dinosaur footprint model
28. Create a drawing of how you think the early dinosaurs may have looked
29. Complete a dinosaur scavenger hunt

Dinosaur Curriculum Web

Social Studies

30. Create a classroom dinosaur newspaper
31. Type student names using a dinosaur font as a header for a dinosaur story
32. Write about how you and your dinosaur spent the day
33. Map out locations where dinosaurs were recently discovered
34. Write and illustrate a Care and Feeding Dinosaur Big Book
35. Role play conflict–resolution scenario
36. Identify, discuss, and create a time line of stops made by the Time Train
37. Share a personal collection
38. Research the life of Mary Anning on the Internet
39. Research Waterhouse Hawkins
40. Discover how fact and fiction combine to create a story
41. Create a chalk drawing of periods in which dinosaurs lived
42. Discuss Internet safety rules

art supplies or a computer drawing program, have students create imaginary dinosaurs with vibrant colors and stripes.

2. Estimate a dinosaur's lifespan: How old were the dinosaurs? (Case #2: An Age-Old Riddle)

This age-old riddle tells us that no one knows for certain how many years the dinosaurs lived. Have students make a birthday card for an imaginary dinosaur, including the dinosaur's age.

3. Investigate how dinosaurs sounded (Case #3: Two-Ton Tooters)

The Magic Tree House research guide explains that paleontologists can only guess which kinds of sounds the dinosaurs made, based on the shape of their heads and bodies. Have students visit Sandia National Laboratories at <www.sandia.gov/media/dinosaur.htm> to find out how digital paleontologists simulated dinosaur sounds. Listen to these computer generated sounds. How did scientists determine how the dinosaurs sounded? Did the size of the dinosaur determine its pitch and tone? Do dinosaurs with longer necks sound different than dinosaurs with short necks? Have students recreate their favorite dinosaur sounds.

4. Go on a fact-finding mission

Have students dig up facts about dinosaurs by going on a scavenger hunt. Copy worksheet figure 1.27.5 *Dinosaur Fact Scavenger Hunt* (see page 33). Allow students to investigate dinosaurs with a partner. The answers can be found in *Dinosaurs*, research guide #1.

5. Compare dinosaur similarities and differences

After looking at chapter one, lead a group discussion comparing dinosaur characteristics. Students record findings on the *Dinosaur Characteristics* worksheet, figure 1.27.75 (see page 34).

6. Create a web of possibilities for what caused dinosaurs to become extinct

What caused the dinosaurs to become extinct? Create a web of possible responses. After looking up "extinct" in the *Dinosaurs* index, have one group read about *The Changing Climate Theory* and the other group read about *The Asteroid Theory*. Have each group debate a theory, supporting it with suggestions for why dinosaurs became extinct. Conclude, by having students vote for the theory, which they now support. Use a spreadsheet program to graph the results.

7. Compare fact with fiction

Compare *Dinosaurs Before Dark* with its nonfiction companion book *Dinosaurs*, noting how one is fiction and the other fact. Have students search *Dinosaurs Before Dark* for examples of fiction and fact. List findings in columns on a chart. How does adding fact to fiction make the story seem believable?

Station Rotations Set up stations throughout the unit to accommodate differentiated learning.

Station 1: *Fine Arts* - Papier-mâché model of a T. rex. After constructing the frame as a class, take turns adding layers of papier-mâché. #3

Station 2: *Social Studies* - Use an index card to record your impressions of the personal collection on display. #37

Station 3: *Language Arts* - Journal a day in the life and times of a dinosaur. #15

Station 4: Science/Technology - Look at *Bones Rock! Everything You Need to Be a Paleontologist* and *Dinosaurs Digs*. Using index cards, describe how footprints are formed. Visit an Overview of Dinosaur Tracking at <http://paleo.cc/paluxy/ovrdino.htm>. #27

Curriculum Connections

Fine Arts/Arts and Crafts

1. Create a Dinosaur Museum

Katie and the Dinosaurs, Mayhew
The Most Amazing Dinosaur, Stevenson
Time Flies, Rohmann
Have students cut the bottom off a jug as shown, and fill the bottom with sand, rocks, or other natural pieces found outdoors. Make or place miniature dinosaurs in the scene to complete the diorama. Students complete a fact card to accompany each exhibit.

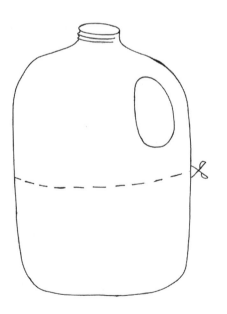

2. Build a Pterosaur model that appears to fly when attached to the ceiling

Fossil, Ewart

Pteranodon: The Life Story of a Pterosaur, Ashby

Pterosaurs: Rulers of the Skies in the Dinosaur Age, Arnold

Have students build a Pterosaur model that appears to fly when attached to the ceiling. Gather information about Pterosaurs at <http://en.wikipedia.org/wiki/Pterosaur#Anatomy>

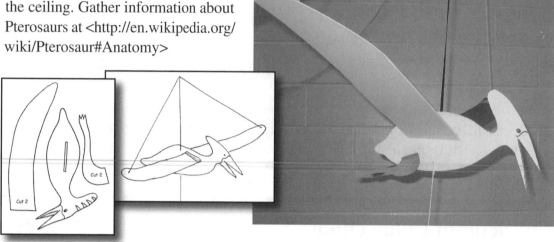

3. Construct a papier-mâché T. rex dinosaur model

T. Rex, French

Construct a large papier-mâché T. rex model dinosaur. Form the dinosaur from cardboard, Styrofoam, crumpled newspaper, balloons, chicken wire, or other construction material. Have students cover the dinosaur form with layers of newspaper strips dipped in a mixture of flour and water or equal parts white glue and water. Paint the completed model when dry.

Joshuasaurus

4. Design a Name-a-saurus

An Alphabet of Dinosaurs, Dodson

After looking at a variety of dinosaurs, have students discuss how they think the dinosaurs got their names. Have students design a *Name-a-saurus* with a computer-drawing program. As an extension, students may write an adventure about their *Name-a-saurus*.

5. Create a clay model Ankylosaurus

Stiff Armor: The Adventures of Ankylosaurus, Dahl
Have each student sculpt an Ankylosaurus from green plasticene clay, using the dinosaur illustration as a study. Cover the shape with eggshell pieces resembling scales and paint the shells with brown and green watercolors. Research why the Ankylosaurus needed scales.

6. Make your own dinosaur bones

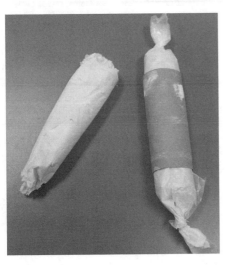

Dinosaur Bones, Barner
Monster Bones: *The Story of a Dinosaur Fossil*, Bailey
Have students roll a piece of waxed paper to line a cardboard tube. Twist the paper at one end so that the plaster will not leak when it is poured into the tube. Have students squeeze each tube to create a unique shape. Mix quick setting plaster. Add food coloring to make the bone a more interesting color. Pour in plaster and twist the end closed. Allow plaster to set for two hours. Unwrap and dry overnight. Bones may be used as sidewalk chalk to create a dinosaur mural.

7. Select a poem to dramatize in a classroom poetry break

Dinosaurs Forever, Wise
Dinosaurs Galore!, Andreae
Tyrannosaurus Was a Beast, Prelutsky
Have each student select a poem and props, such as a dinosaur model, hat, or drawing, to use in performing a poetry break. Emphasize expression and rhythm over memorization.

8. Create a dinostore prop and perform a poetry break

Practice reading "Donald's Dinostore," figure 1.36.5 (see page 35). After working in groups to create cardboard box dinostores filled with items mentioned in the poem, have each group perform a poetry break, using their dinostore as a prop. Discuss which parts of the poem are fiction or fact.

9. Design a shoebox dinosaur bed and discuss bedtime rituals

Dinosnores, DiPucchio
How Do Dinosaurs Say Good Night? Yolen
After selecting a dinosaur from the end pages of
How Do Dinosaurs Say Good Night?, students
design a shoebox bed with a paper dinosaur reading his favorite dinosaur book. Have students
create a two-way dialogue between the dinosaur
and themselves, as they tuck in their baby dinosaur
for the night. Share displays and dialogues noting
bedtime ritual differences.

10. Host a Hollywood Walk of Fame

Albert Goes to Hollywood, Schwartz
Host a Hollywood Walk of Fame, allowing students
to display plaster dinosaur footprints from science
activity #27. As junior paleontologists, have students
describe their imaginary dinosaurs and tell why they
are being recognized as part of Hollywood's Walk
of Fame.

11. Dramatize *All Aboard the Dinotrain*

All Aboard the Dinotrain, Lund
Dramatize the story from *All Aboard the Dinotrain*. While one group reads parts of the story,
the others act it out. At the end of the skit, have the audience guess the meaning of some of
the book's playful dinowords. As an extension, have students create their own dinowords.

Language Arts

12. Create a dinosaur questions flipbook

100 Things You Should Know About Dinosaurs, Parker
Asteroid Impact, Henderson
Dinosaurs, Dixon
Encyclopedia Prehistorica Dinosaurs, Sabuda
My Favorite Dinosaurs, Ashby
As they investigate dinosaurs, ask students to
think about what they want to know about these
creatures of the past and why they became
extinct. Have each student make a flipbook to
fill with questions and answers about dinosaurs.
Share flipbooks with other dinosaur enthusi-
asts.

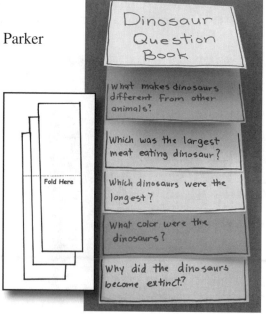

13. Create a travel guide

Dinosaurs Travel: A Guide for Families on the Go, Brown

After reading about the travels of this dinosaur family, have students create a simple cartoon travel guide for dinosaur characters traveling in the past. After deciding upon destinations and mode of transportation, students create an itinerary detailing how long they will spend in each destination and what they will need to pack for the trip.

14. Investigate an author/illustrator

Fossil, Ewart
Time Train, Fleischman

After reading *Fossil* and *Time Train*, have students learn more about author/illustrator Claire Ewart, by visiting her Web site at <www.claireewart.com>.

15. Journal a day in the life and times of a dinosaur

My Dearest Dinosaur, Wild

After reading this story about a mother dinosaur's journal to her absent husband, have students write in their own journals, detailing a day in the life and times of a dinosaur.

16. Write a letter convincing your parents to let you have a pet dinosaur

Can I Have a Stegosaurus, Mom? Can I? Please!?, Grambling
The Care and Feeding of Dinosaurs, Bradley
Dinosaur Dream, Nolan

Have children write convincing letters to their parents, stating reasons why they should be allowed to have a pet dinosaur.

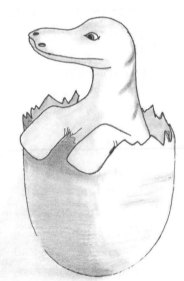

17. Compare *Dinorella* to *Cinderella*

Dinorella: A Prehistoric Fairy Tale, Edwards

Compare *Dinorella* to the traditional story of *Cinderella* on a Venn diagram. As a follow-up, have the class rewrite the traditional *Cinderella* story, setting it in prehistoric times with dinosaur characters. Have students dramatize the story as a skit.

18. Compare *The Dinosaur's New Clothes* to *The Emperor's New Clothes*

The Dinosaur's New Clothes, Goode

Compare *The Dinosaur's New Clothes* to a traditional version of *The Emperor's New Clothes* and a contemporary spin-off version, such as *The Principal's New Clothes*. Document findings on a comparison chart that compares title, characters, setting, storyline, and illustrations.

19. Spin a Yarn

Tyrannosaurus Tex, Birney

After reading *Tyrannosaurus Tex*, research the origin of the expression, *Spin a Yarn*. Spin a yarn about the continued adventures of Tyrannosaurus Tex in a language experience story. Read *The Great Turtle Drive*. Share legendary tall tales, such as *Paul Bunyan* or *Pecos Bill*.

20. Generate questions to investigate planet Earth

Patrick's Dinosaurs on the Internet, Carrick

After reading the book, generate a set of additional questions that Patrick's new friends might be inclined to ask Patrick about his planet, Earth.

Math

21. Calculate and compare dinosaur size differences

Gigantic! How Big Were the Dinosaurs?, O'Brien
Life-Size Dinosaurs, Bergen
Prehistoric Actual Size, Jenkins

Using yarn and a tape measure, have students mark off and compare sizes of some of the dinosaurs discussed in these books. Calculate the size differences of selected dinosaur pairings. Draw a dinosaur to scale with chalk on the playground. How many students fit inside?

22. Compare size of dinosaurs to humans on a pictograph

Gigantic! How Big Were the Dinosaurs?, O'Brien
Life-Size Dinosaurs, Bergen

After reading about dinosaurs of different sizes, copy the *Dinosaur/Human Size Comparison Chart* figure 1.44 (see page 36). Log your findings, comparing the sizes of humans to dinosaurs, found at Zoom Dinosaurs <www.zoomdinosaurs.com>. Have students use a computer-drawing program to create a pictograph of the findings.

T-rex	Stegosaurus	Triceratops	Brachiosaurus	Compsognathus	Apatosaurus

23. Draw a dinosaur footprint to scale

Dinosaurs Walked Here, and Other Stories Fossils Tell, Lauber

Have each student draw a dinosaur footprint to scale. Place dinosaur pictures in the center of a bulletin board. Surround the board with footprints and have students try to match with yarn one another's dinosaur to their footprints.

Science

24. Go on a fact-finding mission and log information about Sue

A Dinosaur Named Sue: The Story of the Colossal Fossil: The World's Most Complete T. Rex, Relf
The Field Mouse and the Dinosaur Named Sue, Wahl

Have students go on a fact-finding mission to gather information about Sue, declared the biggest and most complete T. rex found. Log information on the computer to create a class-room record. Explore the halls of the Field Museum in Chicago at <www.fieldmuseum. org/sue/default.htm>

Assess what students have learned, by having them take the online Sue quiz.

25. Discuss how scientific discoveries have changed dinosaur fact to fiction

Boy, Were We Wrong About Dinosaurs!, Kudlinski

Discuss how modern scientific discoveries have changed what scientists once believed to be fact.

26. Check dinosaur facts for accuracy

Dinosaur Discoveries, Gibbons
New Questions and Answers About Dinosaurs, Simon

Using index cards, record facts found throughout the books. Check the facts against research books for accuracy and place cards in a file box to begin each day with dinosaur trivia.

27. Make a dinosaur footprint model

Bill Nye the Science Guy's Great Big Dinosaur Dig, Nye
Bones Rock! Everything You Need to Know to Be a Paleontologist, Larson
Dinosaur Digs, Quigley

Dampen sand in a sandbox and have students use fingers, fists, or tools to create dinosaur footprint shapes. Pour quick setting plaster into each shape. After it has set, lift the plaster out of the sand and brush off excess sand with a paintbrush. Learn more about making tracks at: <www.drscavanaugh.org/dino/>. To learn more about how dinosaur footprints are formed, view a chart at Overview of Dinosaur Tracking at <http://paleo.cc/paluxy/ovrdino. htm>.

28. Create a drawing of how you think early dinosaurs may have looked

Bones Rock! Everything You Need to Know to Be a Paleontologist, Larson
Digging for Bird-Dinosaurs: An Expedition to Madagascar, Bishop
Dinosaurs All Around: An Artist's View of the Prehistoric World, Arnold
The Dinosaurs of Waterhouse Hawkins, Kerley

Compare pictures of early sculptures of dinosaurs to models today. Discuss changes that have been made over the years, as paleontologists learn more about dinosaurs. Allow students to create individual drawings of how they think the dinosaurs may have looked. Have students research paleontologists to learn how they determine what dinosaurs looked like.

29. Complete a dinosaur scavenger hunt

Patrick's Dinosaurs on the Internet, Carrick

Challenge students to complete a dinosaur scavenger hunt, using the printable dinosaur quiz available at Zoom Dinosaurs at <www.enchantedlearning.com/subjects/dinosaurs>. What are some facts that Patrick should know about his dinosaur friends?

Social Studies

30. Create a classroom dinosaur newspaper

Captain Raptor and the Moon Mystery, O'Malley
Don't Know Much About Dinosaurs, Davis
The News About Dinosaurs, Lauber
Scholastic Dinosaurs A to Z: The Ultimate Dinosaur Encyclopedia, Lessem

Create a classroom dinosaur newspaper covering facts students dig up about dinosaurs. See *Dino Times Worksheet* figure 1.48 (page 37). Guide students to a selection of information books and the Internet to use in their research. Use the *Dinosaur Research Worksheet* figure 1.49 (see page 38) and *Dino Research Rubric* figure 1.50.1 (see page 39). After reading *Captain Raptor and the Moon Mystery* add a short comic strip.

31. Type student names, using a dinosaur font

The News About Dinosaurs, Lauber

Have students type their names using a dinosaur font. Some dinosaur fonts are available for download at Fonts.com <www.fonts.com> or Fontmenu.com <http://www.fontmenu.com/site/_DinosoType.html>.

Other ideas for using dinosaur fonts: Print out the name of your newspaper article report title on sticker paper to use on a dinosaur folder. Use dino font in the header of your story about your dinosaur's adventure, or print out dinosaur names to use on a bulletin board display.

Print out dinosaur names to use on a bulletin board display.

32. Write about how you and your dinosaur spent the day

Danny and the Dinosaur, Hoff

Dinosaur Bob and His Adventures with the Family Lazardo, Joyce

Mrs. Toggle and the Dinosaur, Pulver

After discussing changes they would need to make to accommodate a dinosaur friend, have students write about a day spent with their dinosaur, noting obstacles they overcame.

33. Map out locations where dinosaurs were recently discovered

Dinosaur Discoveries, Gibbons

New Dinos, Tanaka

After listing locations of where dinosaurs were recently discovered, challenge students to find those places on a world map, using yarn to connect dinosaurs with their discovery sites.

34. Write and illustrate a care, feeding, and manners big book

The Care and Feeding of Dinosaurs, Bradley

How Do Dinosaurs Eat Their Food?, Yolen

Write and illustrate a care, feeding, and manners big book based on research, utilizing reference books and the Internet.

35. Role play conflict-resolution scenarios

The Trouble with Tyrannosaurus Rex, Cauley

After reading about how Tyrannosaurus rex bullies others, discuss characteristics of a bully and a victim. How does one enable the other? Guide students to role-play conflict resolution scenarios.

36. Identify, discuss, and create a timeline of stops made by the Time Train

Time Train, Fleischman

After identifying the stops that the Time Train passed through on its way to the time of the dinosaurs, have students create a timeline of those places. Discuss what the class might have encountered had the train dropped them off at one of the earlier destinations. As an extension, have students engage in a creative writing activity, detailing what happens when the Time Train drops them off at an earlier destination.

37. Share a personal collection

Rare Treasure: Mary Anning and Her Remarkable Discoveries, Brown

Stone Girl, Bone Girl: The Story of Mary Anning, Anholt

Ask each student to bring in a personal collection and share reasons for collecting.

38. Research the life of Mary Anning on the Internet

Rare Treasure: Mary Anning and Her Remarkable Discoveries, Brown

Stone Girl, Bone Girl: The Story of Mary Anning, Anholt

Research the life of stone girl, Mary Anning <www.ucmp.berkeley.edu/history/anning.html>. Using the *Anning Research Worksheet*, figure 1.51 (see page 40), have students answer questions to learn about Mary Anning and her contribution to the world of fossils. Discuss how their information checks out with information found in the above picture books.

39. Research Benjamin Waterhouse Hawkins

The Dinosaurs of Waterhouse Hawkins, Kerley

Direct students to use the Internet to find out more about dinosaur artist and sculptor, Benjamin Waterhouse Hawkins at Strange Science <www.strangescience.net/hawkins.htm>.

40. Discover how fact and fiction combine to create a story

Albert Goes to Hollywood, Schwartz

Discover how fact is blended with fiction to create a story. Have students use the Internet and reference books to learn more about the place and location of Wilshire Drive, Santa Monica Beach, Mogo Studios, La Brea Tar Pits, and Mann's Chinese Theater. Pinpoint locations of each site, using a map of the Hollywood area and yarn. Create a classroom travel guide. Students will find these Web sites useful: Western Gateway to Hollywood Boulevard <www.historicla.com/hollywood/block01.html> and Travel for Kids: Hollywood, California <www.travelforkids.com/Funtodo/California/Los_Angeles/hollywood.htm>.

41. Create a chalk drawing of periods in which the dinosaurs lived

The Magic School Bus: In the Time of the Dinosaurs, Cole

Create an outdoor chalk drawing of the time periods in which the dinosaurs lived. Have students draw in dinosaurs that lived in each respective time period.

42. Discuss Internet safety rules

Patrick's Dinosaurs on the Internet, Carrick

Discuss Internet safety rules with students. What are some things that Patrick should do to be safe on the Internet? Brainstorm ideas with the class. For additional safety information, visit: My Rules for Online Safety <www.safekids.com/kidsrules.htm>.

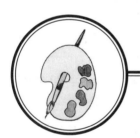

Art Arena

Study Vincent van Gogh (1853-1890) and replicate *The Starry Night*

Vincent van Gogh was a pioneer of modern expressionism and his painting style was very individualized. *The Starry Night* was one of Van Gogh's most famous paintings. Impressionist paintings are often done with wild spontaneous brush strokes, but the strokes in Vincent's painting were laid in with great control. After studying *The Starry Night*, and the illustrations in *Stone Girl, Bone Girl*, allow children to create their own painting of a sky with watered down tempera paints, fingers, and brushes. This is an opportunity for children to create a free flowing expression of what they like about the sky, day or night. Children can learn more about Vincent van Gogh and his paintings through the "How Van Gogh Made His Mark" Web site <http://www.metmuseum.org/explore/van_gogh/intro.html> and the following books:

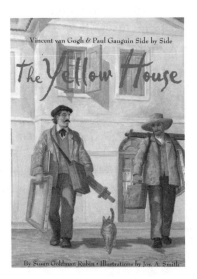

Theme Cuisine

Dinosaur Dig Dirt Pudding
(8 servings)

Ingredients:
24 chocolate sandwich cookies
1 large box chocolate instant pudding
Milk for pudding
32 dinosaur-shaped gummy candies
8 self-sealing sandwich bags

Directions:
Have children make pudding (mud) according to box directions. For each serving, have students: Crush 3 cookies (dirt) in the self-sealing sandwich bag. Layer cookies, 4 dinosaur candies, and pudding in a clear plastic cup.

Dinosaur Bones
(8 Dinosaur Bones)

Courtesy of www.NutritionExplorations.org by the National Dairy Council

Ingredients:

1 cup peanut butter
1 cup dry milk
2 tablespoons honey
8 square graham crackers (finely crushed in self-sealing sandwich bag with rolling pin)

Directions:

Have students combine peanut butter and dry milk. Add the honey and mix well. Divide into equal-size portions. Shape into bones and sprinkle with graham cracker crumbs.

Culminating Activities

Invite parents or another class to visit your *Dinosaur Days Museum*. Create and stamp dinosaur passports to enter the time machine that will transport the class back in time to your *Dinosaur Days Museum*. Have students present a Dino-Cinderella skit, followed by a poetry break. Serve your guests dinosaur theme cuisine. Students serve as tour guides to explain each exhibit. Projects on display may include dioramas, dinosaur boxes, props, suitcases, and papier-mâché dinosaurs. Mark displays with plaster footprints to lead students from one display to another. Display dinosaur journals on a bulletin board. The fact file box could be centrally located in the classroom to serve as a ready source of information for students. Label your displays, bulletin boards, and projects with dinosaur fonts. Display the class artwork inspired by the Vincent van Gogh and *Stone Girl, Bone Girl* activity. Have students share a favorite dinosaur book with their guests.

Dinosaur Assessment Rubric

Students will be able to:	Fair 1	Good 2	Mastered 3	Score
Explain 2 theories of Dinosaur Extinction				
Understand the difference between herbivore and carnivore				
List the names of at least 5 dinosaurs				
Compare the size of some dinosaurs to humans				
Locate dinosaur discoveries on a map				
Identify the periods of time in which dinosaurs lived (Triassic, Jurassic, and Cretaceous)				
Share the contributions of Mary Anning and Waterhouse Hawkins				
Know information about Sue, the Tyrannosaurus rex fossil				
Understand what a fossil is, and how it is formed				

Figure 1.95 Dinosaur Rubric

Multimedia Resources

Digging Up Dinosaurs [video recording]
> by Aliki. T.Y. Crowell Publisher, 1988.
> This video introduces various types of dinosaurs, explaining how scientists find, preserve, and reassemble giant dinosaur skeletons seen in museums (Grades K-2).

Patrick's Dinosaurs [video recording]
> produced by MCA Home Video, 1995.
> When his older brother talks about dinosaurs during a visit to the zoo, Patrick is afraid until he discovers they died out millions of years ago (Grades K-2).

Chicago Field Museum <www.fieldmuseum.org/sue/default.htm>
This is the Chicago Field Museum site about Sue, the largest, most complete, and best-preserved T. rex. Go to the *Just for Kids* section for printable flipbooks and other related activities.

Dinosaur Outpost <http://geocities.com/Hollywood/Academy/5564/outpost.html>
Students can find information and pictures of their favorite dinosaurs in the dinosaur control room. This site has colorful graphics and animation.

Dinosauria On-Line <http://www.dinosauria.com>
This site has an on-line dinosaur encyclopedia including paleontology terms, as well as a photo gallery offering an in-depth scientific view about paleontology.

Dinosaurs: Facts and Fiction <http://pubs.usgs.gov/gip/dinosaurs>
This Web site hosts a collection of new information about dinosaurs that has been acquired over the past 30 years, answering frequently asked questions.

An Overview of Dinosaur Tracking <http://paleo.cc/paluxy/ovrdino.htm>
Basic terms and definitions about fossils, how dinosaur tracks are formed, and a brief history are included in this site that spans the history of dinosaur tracking and includes information, charts, and drawings of dinosaur prints.

Sounds: Dinosaur Sounds <www.sandia.gov/media/dinosaur.htm>
Scientists at Sandia and the New Mexico Museum of Natural History and Science have worked together using computers to simulate the sounds a dinosaur might have made 75 million years ago.

Strange Science <www.strangescience.net/hawkins.htm>
Biographical information about Benjamin Waterhouse Hawkins and his early dinosaur illustrations are found at this site.

ZoomDinosaurs.com <www.enchantedlearning.com/subjects/dinosaurs>
A great resource for grades 2-12, this site features dinosaur information sheets, quizzes, word scrambles, printable worksheets, and even dinosaur math activities.

Book Resources

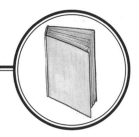

Fiction Books

Albert Goes to Hollywood
by Henry Schwartz. Illus. Amy Schwartz. Orchard Books, 1992.
When eight-year-old Liz Bradford returns from a camping trip with a living dinosaur, she helps Albert find a job as a movie star to support his excessive appetite (Grades K-2).

All Aboard the Dinotrain
by Deb Lund. Illus. Howard Fine. Harcourt, Inc., 2006.
A group of adventure seeking dinosaurs survives a series of mishaps as they travel up and down hills on a rollicking roller coaster train ride (Grades K-2).

Can I Have a Stegosaurus, Mom? Can I? Please!?
by Lois Grambling. Illus. H. B. Lewis.
Troll Associates: Bridgewater Books, 1995.
As a child pleads his case for being allowed to have a pet stegosaurus, the egg he has been sitting on hatches and a shadow provides a clue as to what is yet to come (Grades K-2).

Captain Raptor and the Moon Mystery
by Kevin O'Malley. Illus. Patrick O'Brien. Walker and Company, 2005.
When an unidentified flying object crashes into the planet Jurassica, the interstellar hero, Captain Raptor, and his crew investigate. After learning that Captain Storm's ship was struck down by a meteor shower, he finds a way to help his new found alien (human) friends (Grades 1-3).

The Care and Feeding of Dinosaurs
by Timothy J. Bradley. The Millbrook Press, 2000.
Should I give my dinosaur a bath? How big will my dinosaur become? Tongue-in-cheek answers combining fact with fiction are the result of this whimsical dinosaur care book (Grades K-3).

Danny and the Dinosaur
by Syd Hoff. HarperCollins, 1958/1999.
After befriending a dinosaur in the museum, Danny and his friend spend the day together (Grades K-2).

Dinorella: A Prehistoric Fairy Tale

by Pamela Duncan Edwards. Illus. Henry Cole. Hyperion Books for Children, 1997.
When Dinorella rescues the duke from the dreaded Deinonychus by hurling a diamond at his dentures, the duke goes in search of the dinosaur wearing the dazzling jewel (Grades 1-3).

Dinosaur Bob and His Adventures with the Family Lazardo

by William Joyce. Harper& Row, 1988.
The Lazardo family returns from an African vacation with a dinosaur that is embraced by everyone, until he is arrested for disturbing the peace (Grades K-2).

Dinosaur Bones

by Bob Barner. Chronicle Books, 2001.
A poem running from page to page forms the core of this story about dinosaur bones, showcasing interesting dinosaur facts with vibrant illustrations (Grades K-2).

Dinosaur Dream

by Dennis Nolan. Simon & Schuster Books for Young Readers, 1990.
When a baby Apatosaurus awakens Wilber, he travels back in time to return the baby dinosaur to its own time period (Grades K-3).

The Dinosaur's New Clothes

by Diane Goode. Scholastic, 1999.
In this spin-off of Andersen's classic fairy tale, the emperor is more interested in being fashionable than taking care of his responsibilities as a ruler. Life at Versailles is presented through dinosaurs donning powdered wigs and period costumes rendered in pastels (Grades K-3).

Dinosaurs Travel: A Guide for Families on the Go

by Laurie Krasny Brown and Marc Brown. Little Brown and Company: Joy Street Books, 1988.
Comical dinosaur characters and humorous text guide young readers through the travel process, emphasizing where to go, how to pack, and ways in which to memorialize the trip (Grades K-2).

Dinosnores

by Kelly DiPucchio. Illus. Ponder Goembel. HarperCollins Publishers, 2005.
This fanciful adventure explains how the snoring of gigantic dinosaurs caused cracking and splitting of a super continent, resulting in landforms common today (Grades K-2).

The Field Mouse and the Dinosaur Named Sue

by Jan Wahl. Illus. Bob Doucet. Scholastic, Inc. and the Field Museum, 2000.
When a small mouse living in South Dakota discovers his bone constructed roof missing,

his search for the lost bone takes him to the Field Museum in Chicago where he encounters Sue, the largest and most complete T. rex (Grades K-2).

Fossil

by Claire Ewart. Walker & Company, 2004.
When a young girl finds a special stone, she imagines how the Pterosaur lived, died, and is eventually fossilized into stone. Lyrical text and vibrant watercolors are followed by an in-depth explanation of fossil evidence (Grades K-2).

Katie and the Dinosaurs

by James Mayhew. Bantam Books, 1992.
Katie ventures through a "No Admittance" door in the Natural History Museum, where she learns all about dinosaurs as she assists Hadrosaurus in locating his parents (Grades K-2).

The Magic School Bus: In the Time of the Dinosaurs

by Joanna Cole. Illus. Bruce Degen. Scholastic Inc., 1994.
Ms. Frizzle's class is transported to prehistoric times where they get a first hand experience of what it was like to live in a time of dinosaurs (Grades K-3).

The Most Amazing Dinosaur

by James Stevenson. Greenwillow Books, 2000.
When Wilfred the rat stumbles upon a museum, the unofficial residents give him a chaotic tour that results in their eviction, until the museum inspector discovers their artwork (Grades K-2).

Mrs. Toggle and the Dinosaur

by Robin Pulver. Illus. R. W. Alley. Macmillan Publishing Company, 1991.
After making all sorts of accommodations for her new student, Mrs. Toggle is surprised to learn that the student is not a dinosaur but rather a little girl named Dina Sawyer (Grades K-2).

My Dearest Dinosaur

by Margaret Wild. Illus. Donna Rawlins. Orchard Books, 1992.
In a series of letters to her absent mate, a mother dinosaur journals day to day activities as she struggles to find a safe home for her babies (Grades K-2).

Patrick's Dinosaurs on the Internet

by Carol Carrick. Illus. David Milgrim. Clarion Books: Houghton Mifflin Company, 1999.
After researching dinosaurs on the Internet, Patrick is awakened by a dinosaur that transports him to his planet for Show and Tell (Grades K-2).

Time Flies

by Eric Rohmann. Crown Publishers, Inc., 1994.
In this wordless tale, a small bird enjoys exploring every aspect of a dinosaur exhibit until the dinosaurs appear to come to life and one views the bird as its next meal (Grades K-2).

Time Train

by Paul Fleischman. Illus. Claire Ewart. HarperCollins, 1991.
A class trip by way of the Rocky Mountain Unlimited takes an unexpected turn, transporting its passengers through time periods spanning Civil War days to dinosaurs. Students enjoy cooking a dinosaur egg, gliding on pterodactyls, and playing ball with dinosaurs (Grades K-3).

T. Rex

by Vivian French. Illus. Alison Bartlett. Candlewick Press, 2004.
What do we really know about T. rex and how much is based on theories or educated guesses? Subject matter is covered in a questioning format with acrylic painted illustrations (Grades K-2).

The Trouble with Tyrannosaurus Rex

by Lorinda Bryan Cauley. Harcourt Brace Jovanovich, 1988.
When a T. rex threatens to gobble up all of the dinosaurs in the neighborhood, Duckbill and Ankylosaurus devise a plan to outwit the bully (Grades K-3).

Tyrannosaurus Tex

by Betty G. Birney. Illus. John O'Brien. Houghton Mifflin Company, 1994.
In this modern day legend told around a campfire, a dinosaur cowboy, known as Tyrannosaurus Tex, helps cowboys put out a brush fire and scare lowdown rustlers away (Grades K-3).

Poetry Books

Dinosaurs Forever

by William Wise. Illus. Lynn Munsinger. Dial Books for Young Readers, 2000.
Dino-rhymes and nonsense poems about the world of dinosaurs are brought to life through humorous illustrations rendered in pastel watercolors (Grades 1-4).

Dinosaurs Galore!

by Giles Andreae. Illus. David Wojtowycz. Tiger Tales, 2005.
Through quirky pictures and lively rhymes, dinosaurs introduce themselves in a descriptive poem that ends in the sleepy dinosaurs bidding the reader goodnight (Grades K-2).

How Do Dinosaurs Eat Their Food?

by Jane Yolen. Illus. Mark Teague. Scholastic: The Blue Sky Press, 2005.
Through clever antics and humorous characters, this book of manners questions what kind of manners dinosaurs would use to eat their food. End pages depict dining dinosaurs (Grades K-2).

How Do Dinosaurs Say Good Night?

by Jane Yolen. Illus. Mark Teague. Scholastic: The Blue Sky Press, 2000.
Readers are given a fanciful look into the bedtime rituals of dinosaur children and their parents, through lyrical text and humorous pictures (Grades K-2).

Tyrannosaurus Was a Beast

by Jack Prelutsky. Illus. Arnold Lobel. Greenwillow Books, 1988.
Fourteen humorous dinosaur poems, spanning Tyrannosaurus to Seismosaurus, are enhanced by playful watercolor illustrations (Grades K-4).

Information Books

100 Things You Should Know About Dinosaurs

by Steve Parker. Mason Crest Publishers, 2001.
Did you know that diplodocus could crack its tail like a whip to ward off enemies? When did the dinosaurs die out? Dinosaur enthusiasts will welcome this potpourri of dinosaur facts and questions (Grades K-4).

An Alphabet of Dinosaurs

by Peter Dodson. Illus. Wayne D. Barlowe. Scholastic, 1995.
The latest facts about 26 familiar dinosaurs are revealed through bold paintings, interesting facts, and descriptive paragraphs (Grades K-3).

Asteroid Impact

by Douglas Henderson. Penguin Putnam Inc.: Dial Books for Young Readers, 2000.
Theorizing that the collision of an asteroid with earth resulted in the extinction of dinosaurs, Henderson recreates the sequence of events following the asteroid's impact (Grades 2-6).

Bill Nye the Science Guy's Great Big Dinosaur Dig

by Bill Nye and Ian G. Saunders. Illus. Michael Koelsch. Hyperion Books for Children, 2002.

This television celebrity introduces facts about dinosaurs through humor and experimentation, such as an activity that determines how much weight a dinosaur's body can carry (Grades 1-4).

Bones Rock! Everything You Need to Know to Be a Paleontologist

by Peter Larson and Kristin Donnan. Invisible Cities Press, 2004.

In a book that goes right to the dig and shares the experience in photo-essay format, readers learn how evidence is collected, what to do with a fossil, and how paleontologists rely on the scientific method to come to conclusions (Grades 4-8).

Boy, Were We Wrong About Dinosaurs!

by Kathleen V. Kudlinski. Illus. S. D. Schindler. Dutton Children's Books, 2005.

This book discusses how common ideas about dinosaurs are changing, as scientists find new ways to unearth information from the past (Grades K-4).

Digging for Bird-Dinosaurs: An Expedition to Madagascar

by Nic Bishop. Houghton Mifflin Company, 2000.

The experiences of a paleontologist and her team, who traveled to Madagascar in search of fossil birds in 1998, are revealed through large full-color photographs and engaging text (Grades 3-6).

Dinosaur Digs

by Mary Quigley. Heinemann Library, 2006.

The basics of paleontology, types of dinosaurs, and fossil evidence are just some of the topics covered in this well written text. Special features include maps, timelines, a glossary, and engaging full color photographs (Grades 2-6).

Dinosaur Discoveries

by Gail Gibbons. Holiday House, 2005.

Dinosaur discoveries and current theories about the history of dinosaurs are introduced with a focus on dinosaurs living in the Triassic, Jurassic, and Cretaceous periods (Grades K-3).

A Dinosaur Named Sue: The Story of the Colossal Fossil: The World's Most Complete T. Rex

by Pat Relf, with the SUE Science Team of the Field Museum.

Scholastic Inc., 2000.
Through photographs and descriptive text, the story of the fossil find of the century is told, documenting Sue's excavation and reconstruction (Grades 3-8).

Dinosaurs

by Dougal Dixon. DK Publishing, Inc., 2003.
Detailed information about dinosaurs, accompanied by cross-sections and transparent layers, introduces dinosaur enthusiasts to sights such as a T. rex restoration (Grades 2-6).

Dinosaurs All Around: An Artist's View of the Prehistoric World

by Caroline Arnold. Photographs by Richard Hewett. Clarion Books, 1993.
By making a visit to the studio of sculptors Stephen and Sylvia Czerkas, the reader learns how fossil remains are pieced together, revealing what dinosaurs were really like (Grades 2-4).

The Dinosaurs of Waterhouse Hawkins

by Barbara Kerley. Illus. Brian Selznick. Scholastic Press, 2001.
This picture book biography highlights the artist and lecturer, Benjamin Waterhouse Hawkins, whose dinosaur sculptures introduced the world to the first life-sized dinosaur models (Grades 2-4).

Dinosaurs Walked Here, and Other Stories Fossils Tell

by Patricia Lauber. Bradbury Press, 1986.
Through text and color photographs, this book looks at a variety of plant and animal fossils, leaving a record of the prehistoric world (Grades 2-6).

Don't Know Much About Dinosaurs

by Kenneth C. Davis. Illus. Pedro Martin. HarperCollins Publishers, 2004.
Typical questions about dinosaurs, such as "Were dinosaurs the first living things on earth?" or "How did the dinosaurs die out?" are addressed in a lively manner (Grades K-3).

Encyclopedia Prehistorica Dinosaurs

by Robert Sabuda and Matthew Reinhart. Candlewick Press, 2005.
Full of facts and trivia, information about more than 50 species of dinosaurs is conveyed through amazing pop-up dinosaurs and informational flaps (Grades K-4).

Gigantic! How Big Were the Dinosaurs?

by Patrick O'Brien. Henry Holt and Company, 1999.
This visual book emphasizes size and special dinosaur features by pairing them with pictures of large present day items such as a steam shovel (Grades K-2).

Life-Size Dinosaurs

by David Bergen. Sterling Publishing Company, Inc., 2004.
This introduction to the world of dinosaurs includes foldout pages that reveal dinosaur parts to help children visualize how big a footprint or T. rex's teeth actually were (Grades 1-4).

Monster Bones: The Story of a Dinosaur Fossil

by Jacqui Bailey. Illus. Matthew Lilly. Picture Window Books, 2004.
The story of a dinosaur fossil, from its death caused by a fall from a riverbank to the bones eventual change to stone, are told in lively format with comical illustrations (Grades 1-4).

My Favorite Dinosaurs

by Ruth Ashby. Illus. John Sibbick. Simon & Schuster: Milk and Cookies Press, 2005.
John Sibbick's paintings of dinosaurs introduced in groups form the basis of this book, accompanied by facts and a description of each scene (Grades K-3).

New Dinos

by Shelley Tanaka. Illus. Alan Barnard. Madison Press Book: An Atheneum Book for Young Readers, 2002.
Readers are introduced to recently discovered dinosaurs spanning Madagascar, China, and South America. Discussions include dinosaur sounds and color to extinction theories (Grades 1-4).

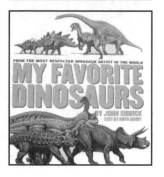

New Questions and Answers About Dinosaurs

by Seymour Simon. Illus. Jennifer Dewey, Morrow Junior Books, 1990.
This informative book addresses a potpourri of questions and answers about dinosaurs such as, "Which dinosaur had the biggest head?" or "What colors were the dinosaurs?" (Grades K-3).

The News About Dinosaurs

by Patricia Lauber. Macmillan Company: Bradbury Press: Aladdin Books, 1994.
Through a series of essays and up-to-date paintings and drawings by artists with a background in paleontology, Lauber introduces scientific thinking about dinosaurs (Grades 2-4).

Prehistoric Actual Size

by Steve Jenkins. Houghton Mifflin, 2005.
Jenkins offers a look at prehistoric animals spanning the Velociraptor to the cockroach through minimal text and life-size collages of body parts (Grades K-3).

Pteranodon: The Life Story of a Pterosaur

by Ruth Ashby. Illus. Phil Wilson. Harry N. Abrams, Inc., 2005.
The adventures of a Pterosaur from birth to fatherhood unfolds, incorporating life lessons with warnings such as not to sleep on the cliffs, or to avoid T. rex (Grades K-2).

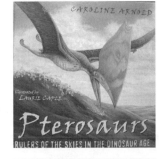

Pterosaurs: Rulers of the Skies in the Dinosaur Age

by Caroline Arnold. Illus. Laurie Caple. Clarion Books, 2004.
Pterosaurs, how their bodies were built for flight, fossil discoveries, and more are found in this book brought to life through vividly colored illustrations (Grades K-3).

Rare Treasure: Mary Anning and Her Remarkable Discoveries

by Don Brown. Houghton Mifflin Company, 1999.
This picture book biography of one of the first commercial fossil collectors, discusses how an English girl was inspired by the discovery of an Ichthyosaur fossil, at a young age (Grades K-3).

Scholastic Dinosaurs A to Z: The Ultimate Dinosaur Encyclopedia

by Don Lessem. Illus. Jan Sovak. Scholastic Inc., 2003.
This comprehensive guide provides information and answers questions about an extensive selection of dinosaurs from A to Z (Grades 2-8).

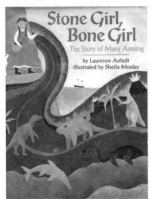

Stiff Armor: The Adventure of Ankylosaurus

by Michael Dahl. Illus. Garry Nichols. Picture Window Books, 2005.
While running away from an erupting volcano, the plant eating Ankylosaurus is confronted by a more serious danger as he encounters the meat eating T. rex in his path (Grades K-3).

Stone Girl, Bone Girl: The Story of Mary Anning

by Laurence Anholt. Illus. Sheila Moxley. Orchard Books, 1998.
The discovery of an Ichthyosaur skeleton at a young age leads to a lifelong interest in fossil hunting for Mary Anning, as depicted in this picture book biography (Grades K-3).

Activity Books

Dinomania: Things to Do with Dinosaurs

by Mick Manning and Brita Granstrom. Holiday House, 2002.
Dinomaniacs learn about different types of dinosaurs living during the Jurassic period as they engage in theme-related projects, such as making a Pterosaur mobile (Grades 2-5).

Paper Dinosaurs

by Alan Folder. Illus. Maureen Galvani. Scholastic and Tangerine Press, 2000.
Paper-folding techniques are used to create a variety of paper dinosaurs (Grades 2-6).

Ralph Masiello's Dinosaur Drawing Book

by Ralph Masiello. Charlesbridge Publishing, 2005.
Ralph Masiello offers simple strategies for drawing dinosaurs that include a Challenge Steps section for embellishing drawings (Grades 1-4).

Worksheets and Templates

Dear _____ ,

_____

                                        To:

_____

_____

_____

_____

_____

_____

Figure 1.23 Postcard Template Blank

Name _____

Dinosaur Fact
Scavenger Hunt

1. All dinosaurs lived during the _____ Era.

2. What are the three periods of time that dinosaurs lived?

   _____

   _____

   _____

3. _____ are any traces of life from a long-ago age.

4. What are sets of dinosaur footprints going the same way called? _____

   _____

5. What does the word dinosaur mean in Greek? _____

   _____

6. Name the two paleontologists whose bone battles lasted twenty years, and led
   to the discovery of over 130 different dinosaurs.

   _____   _____

Figure 1.27.5 Dinosaur Fact Scavenger Hunt

Name _____

Dinosaur Characteristics

Ways they were alike   Ways they were different

1. _____   1. _____

2. _____   2. _____

3. _____   3. _____

4. _____   4. _____

5. _____   5. _____

6. _____   6. _____

7. _____   7. _____

8. _____   8. _____

Figure 1.27.75 Dinosaur Characteristics

Donald's Dinostore

By Steve Presser

Donald learned about the brontosaurus,
The stegosaurus, and the tyrannosaurus.
Which ones eat veggies, and which ones eat meat,
And which ones grow to a hundred feet.

He studied their skin, and studied their size,
And studied their mouths, ears, noses, and eyes.
Until one day he thought, "I can learn no more!"
And decided to open a dinostore.

He made dinosaur bowls as big as pools,
Ninety-foot tables and fifty-foot stools,
Dress pants the size of six elephants,
Giant tuxedos for special events.

He knew dinosaurs like the back of his hand,
But nothing was going as he had planned.
"Dinosaurs should like all these things!" he said,
As he chewed on his pencil and scratched his head.

"What's that you say?" Donald cleaned out his ears.
"You say dinosaurs have been dead for years?"
His jaw dropped open and poor Donald blinked
As his huge dinostore became extinct.

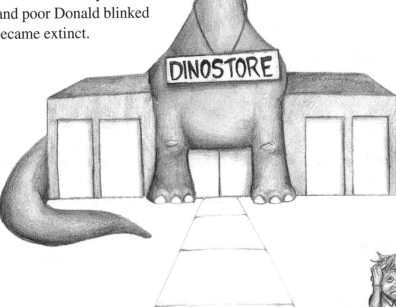

Figure 1.36.5 Donald's Dinostore Poem

Dinosaur /Human
Size Comparison Chart

Name _____

Fill in this chart using information found at
www.zoomdinosaurs.com

Dinosaur Name	Height (use tallest height)	Weight	Type of Food Plant or meat-eater	How many humans tall? (human=6ft.)
Tyrannosaurus rex				
Stegosaurus				
Triceratops				
Brachiosaurus				
Compsognathus				
Apatosaurus (Brontosaurus)				

Which dinosaur is the tallest? _____

Which dinosaur is the shortest? _____

Which dinosaur weighs the most? _____

Figure 1.44 Dinosaur Size Comparison Chart

Figure 1.48 Dino Times Worksheet

Dinosaur Research Sheet

Use a selection of dinosaur books or the Internet (www.zoomdinosaurs.com) to find the following information about your assigned dinosaur.

The name of your dinosaur _____

1. Was your dinosaur a carnivore (meat-eater) or herbivore (plant-eater)? _____

2. In which time period did your dinosaur live?

_____

3. Did your dinosaur have two legs or four legs?
_____

4. Where did your dinosaur live?
_____

5. What size was your dinosaur?
_____

List the sources where you found your information.

    1. _____

    2. _____

    3. _____

Figure 1.49 Dinosaur Research Sheet

Dino Research Rubric

	Beginning 1	Developing 2	Accomplished 3
Research	Inadequate information	Most information found	Information complete 3 sources listed
Spelling/ grammar	Many errors	Few errors	Proofread No errors
Presentation	Difficult to read	Legible writing	Neatly completed
Drawing	Incomplete	Drawing complete Not colored	Drawing complete Colored

Figure 1.50.1 Dino Research Rubric

Researching the Life of Mary Anning

Name _____

www.enchantedlearning.com/subjects/dinosaurs/glossary/Anning.shtml

1. In what year was Mary Anning born? _____

2. How old was Mary Anning when she died? _____

(hint: subtract the year she was born from the year she died)

3. Why did Mary decide to collect fossils?

_____

4. Who helped her collect fossils?

_____

5. Where did Mary Anning live? _____

6. The cliffs in Lyme Regis contained fossil layers from which three time periods?

_____   _____   _____

7. Mary Anning found and prepared the first fossilized

_____ and the first_____.

Figure 1.51 Anning Research

From *Curriculum Connections for Tree House Travelers for Grades K-4* by Jane Berner, Sabrina Minser, and Helen Burkart Presser. Columbus, OH: Linworth Publishing, Inc. Further reproduction prohibited. Copyright © 2008.

UNIT 2
Destination Medieval Times

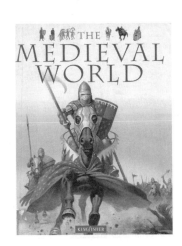

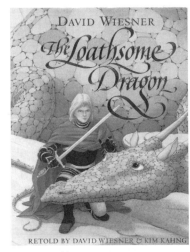

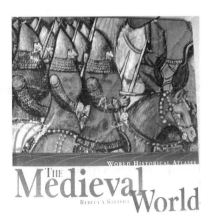

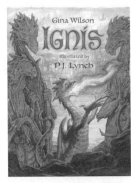

Travel Itinerary

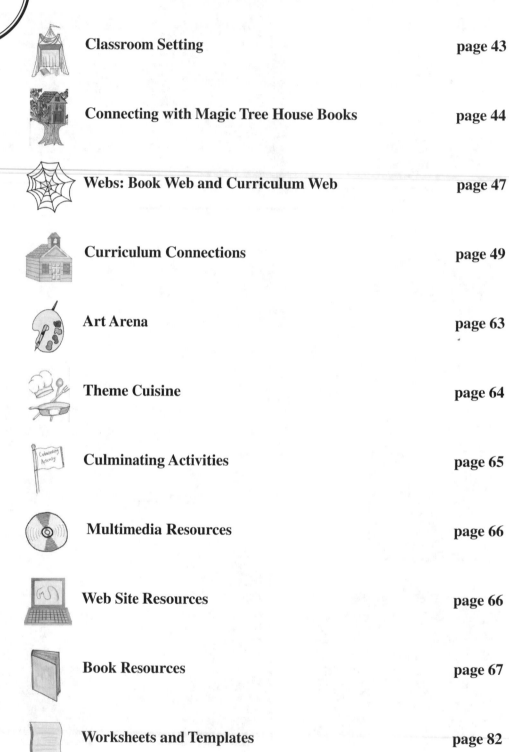

Classroom Setting

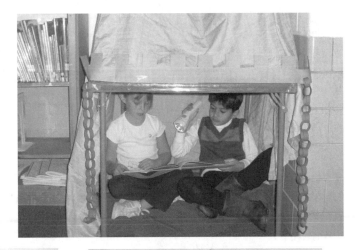

Classroom Setting Supplies

- card table
- sheet
- crown
- scepter
- paper chain for drawbridge
- construction cones for castle top
- castle flags
- armor
- family crest

Word Wall

Middle Ages	kingdom
Medieval period	castle
lord	bailey
lady	siege
page	moat
serf	chivalry
dungeon	jester
feudal system	troubadours
knight	tournament

Magic Tree House Book Annotations

The Knight at Dawn

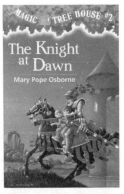

by Mary Pope Osborne. Illus. Sal Murdocca. Random House, 1993.
Jack and Annie travel back in time to the Middle Ages, where they observe a medieval feast taking place in the great hall. When a man carrying pies sees them, they run down the hall and end up in the armory. There, they are captured by guards and thrown into a dungeon, accused of being spies. Annie frightens the guards with her flashlight and the two escape through winding passages, ending up in the moat. They swim to safety and are rescued by the knight on a black horse that they saw when they first arrived. They ride with him on his horse to the tree house that takes them back to their home in Frog Creek, Pennsylvania (Grades K-3).

Knights and Castles

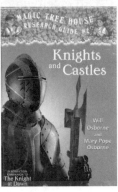

by Will Osborne and Mary Pope Osborne. Illus. Sal Murdocca. Random House, 2000.
This nonfiction companion to *The Knight at Dawn* is Jack and Annie's research guide to the Middle Ages. Castle life, festivals and fairs, knights, armor, weapons, battles, and sieges are all part of the fare. An afterword includes resources for further study (Grades K-3).

The Knight at Dawn Critical Thinking Questions

1. What did Jack and Annie disagree about when they first arrived in medieval times?
2. What was the purpose of the windmill that Jack and Annie saw before they entered the castle?
3. Where did the medieval feast take place in the castle and what is a medieval feast?
4. Why do you suppose the castle guards were afraid of Annie's flashlight?
5. What significance did the blue bookmark hold for Jack and Annie?

The Knight at Dawn Curriculum Connections

1. List places to visit

Instruct students to make a list of time periods and places they would like to go if they discovered a tree house like Jack and Annie. Have students select their top choice and describe what they would like to see and do when they arrive at their destination.

2. Write a descriptive paragraph

Have students write a paragraph describing the kind of person they would choose to accompany them on their travels. Would this friend be cautious like Jack or adventurous like Annie? What attributes should a travel mate possess? Have students consider what qualities would make them a good travel partner?

3. Design an alternative book cover

After reading the *Knight at Dawn* with your class have students plan and design an alternative cover illustration. Develop ideas based on the content of the book.

4. Research the weight of a helmet

Fill each of two plastic bags with five pounds of sand. Have students take turns placing the bags on their shoulders, and walk around the classroom for one minute. Work with students to calculate the number of bags it would take to equal the weight of a 40-pound helmet. Research the weight of full armor.

5. Investigate peacocks on the Internet

As Jack and Annie learned, medieval cooks would serve peacocks during a feast. Have students investigate peacocks using *Peacock Research*, figure 2.19 (see page 82).

6. Juggle like a court jester

Collect three or four small soft balls or lightweight scarves for students to practice juggling. Make sure they are small enough to handle two in their hand at once. Visit Chris Seguin's Juggling Page, which is an animated Web site at <www.acm.uiuc.edu/webmonkeys/juggling>.

7. Balance a pole

Jack and Annie observed jesters entertaining the crowd by balancing poles on their palms. Cut a ¾ inch dowel rod about 18 inches long. This size is long enough to balance easily. Guide students as they take turns balancing the rod on their palm.

Knights and Castles Curriculum Connections

1. Research inventions of the time

Compare the comfort of modern appliances to what the kings and queens had in their castles. Brainstorm how life would have been different if modern day appliances were introduced to the people of the Middle Ages. Ask students which modern day inventions they would take with them and why. Compile a list of inventions that were created during the Middle Ages. Use the Inventions in the Middle Ages Web site <www.middle-ages.org.uk/inventions-in-the-middle-ages.htm> to help.

2. Describe events leading to a battle

Page 15 in the research guide shows a painting of a medieval war scene. After looking at paintings of similar war scenes in books and on the Internet, discuss events that lead up to the battles. Is war necessary? Have students take a stance and debate the pros and cons of war.

3. Compile information about the feudal system

Review information about the feudal system on pages 16 thru 19 in the research guide. As a class, make a list of jobs available as part of the feudal system and explain how the system worked.

4. Design a masterpiece to present to the guild

Castle building involved the skills of masons, carpenters, and blacksmiths, as detailed on page 27 of the research guide. Let students decide which job would be best for them, and design a plan or project to present to the guild to become a master craftsman.

5. Compare stone castles to wooden castles

Gather a bucket full of small rocks or pea gravel. Help students mix plaster with dirt to give the plaster color and texture. Cement the stones together with the mixture to build a stone castle on a box form. Build a wooden castle using craft sticks. Discuss attributes and drawbacks of each building and evaluate which would be safer.

6. Hold a chess tournament

Students will find the Chess Is Fun Web site <www.princeton.edu/~jedwards/cif/intro.html> helpful in learning to play chess. Hold several chess matches while students learn the game, culminating in a class chess tournament.

7. Investigate the origin of nursery rhymes

Chapter 4, "Castle Life," in the research guide depicts a feast with birds flying out of a pie. Have students investigate the origin of *Sing a Song of Sixpence* to see if there is a connection to the Middle Ages. As an extension, research other nursery rhymes such as *London Bridge,* and *Here We Go Round the Mulberry Bush,* to see if there is a connection to medieval history.

8. Create a poster of knights' armor

Chapter 7 of the research guide discusses armor. Divide the class into small groups and have each group create a poster displaying and labeling armor a knight and his horse would wear during tournaments. Decorate your poster. Challenge students to learn why each piece of armor was important. For a detailed diagram go to Armour Diagrams at <www.beautifuliron.com/armour_diagrams.htm> or Armor Worksheet at <www.sbceo.k12.ca.us./%7Evms/carlton/page11.htm>.

STATION ROTATIONS - Set up stations throughout the unit to accommodate differentiated learning.

Station 1: *Fine Arts* - Use calligraphy markers to copy a short passage from a book. Illuminate the first letter. #3

Station 2: *Social Studies* - Take a virtual tour of gargoyles to learn how they were created and where they are located. Visit Gargoyles & Grotesques at <http://www.stonecarver.com/gargoyle.html>. #53

Station 3: *Language Arts* - Write a letter to your parents apologizing for the chaos your pet dragon caused, after sneaking it into school for the day. #29

Station 4: *Fine Arts/Music* - Listen to medieval music while designing a stained glass window. For CD information, refer to the multimedia section. #2

Curriculum Connections

Fine Arts/Arts and Crafts

1. Design a town seal

Castles, Steele
Medieval Towns, Trade, and Travel, Elliot
The Medieval World, Steele

Students mix quick setting plaster and pour ½ inch plaster into small paper cups. Set up over night. Pop out the plaster disk and have students carve a design into the plaster. Place aluminum foil over the disk and press hard enough to make the foil descend into the carved grooves. Have students stamp their town seal into sealing wax and use it to seal official letters.

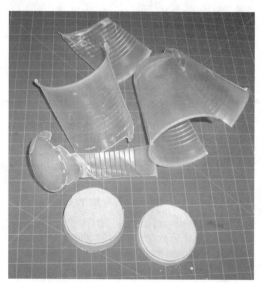

Medieval Fiction Books

Adventures in the Middle Ages, *Bailey*	
The Adventures of Robin Hood, *McSpadden*	6
The Adventures of Robin Hood, *Williams*	6
Arthur and the Sword, *Sabuda*	2
Behold…the Dragons, *Gibbons*	7
Chanticleer and the Fox, *Chaucer*	32
The Dragon and the Unicorn, *Cherry*	5, 34
Dragonology: The Complete Book of Dragons, *Steer*	31, 41
The Dragonology Handbook: A Practical Course in Dragons, *Steer*	18, 31, 41
Dragons, *Penner*	29, 41
The Dwarf, the Giant, and the Unicorn, *Giblin*	51
The Egg, *Robertson*	29
Favorite Medieval Tales, *Osborne*	22, 32
Fighting Knights, *Wright*	
Good Night, Good Knight, *Thomas*	19
Ignis, *Wilson*	29
Imagine You're a Knight, *Clibbon*	33, 50, 51
Joan of Arc, *Poole*	28
Joan of Arc, *Stanley*	28
King Arthur and the Knights of the Round Table, *Williams*	21
The Kiss that Missed, *Melling*	26
The Kitchen Knight: A Tale of King Arthur, *Hodges*	33
The Knight and the Dragon, *dePaola*	18
The Loathsome Dragon, *Wiesner*	18
A Medieval Feast, *Aliki*	24
Medieval Myths, Legends, and Songs, *Trembinski*	11, 27
Merlin and the Making of the King, *Hodges*	5
Ms. Frizzle's Adventures: Medieval Castle, *Cole*	16
Night of the Gargoyles, *Bunting*	53
Pondlarker, *Gwynne*	25
The Princess Knight, *Funke*	44
Princess Smartypants, *Cole*	
The Reluctant Dragon, *Grahame*	18
Saint George and the Dragon, *Hodges*	5
The Secret in the Matchbox, *Willis*	29
Simeon's Gift, *Edwards*	
Sir Cedric, *Gerrard*	
Sir Cumference and the First Round Table, *Neuschwander*	39
Tales of King Arthur: Excalibur, *Talbott*	21
Tales of King Arthur: The Sword in the Stone, *Talbott*	21, 51
A Tournament of Knights, *Lasker*	8, 13

Medieval Information Books

Archers, Alchemists, and 98 Other Medieval Jobs You Might Have Loved or Loathed, *Galloway*	35
Arts and Literature in the Middle Ages, *Cels*	2, 3, 5, 11
Castle: Medieval Days and Nights, *Olmon*	15
Castles, *Steele*	1, 42
Children and Games in the Middle Ages, *Elliott*	10, 52
Clothes and Crafts in the Middle Ages, *Dawson*	4, 12, 13
Clothing in the Middle Ages, *Elliott*	8, 9
Days of the Knights: A Tale of Castles and Battles, *Maynard*	45
Famous People of the Middle Ages, *Trembinski*	28
Food and Feasts in the Middle Ages, *Elliott*	
In the Time of Knights, *Tanaka*	
Knights, *Steele*	16, 26
Knights and Heroes, *Hamilton*	16, 17, 33
Knights in Shining Armor, *Gibbons*	15, 16, 17
The Life in a Castle, *Eastwood*	49
Life in a Medieval Monastery, *Cels*	5, 20
Life on a Medieval Manor, *Cels*	52
Life of a Knight, *Eastwood*	43
A Medieval Castle, *Bergin*	14, 15
A Medieval Castle, *Gresko*	42, 45
Medieval Muck, *Dobson*	
Medieval Society, *Eastwood*	20
Medieval Towns, Trade, and Travel, *Elliott*	1, 37, 48
The Medieval World, *Steele*	1, 17, 23, 26, 42, 50
The Medieval World, *Stefoff*	23, 40
The Middle Ages, *Corbishley*	2
The Middle Ages, *Quigley*	23, 30
Peasant, *Lily*	46
Places of Worship in the Middle Ages, *Eastwood*	2, 38
Science and Technology in the Middle Ages, *Findon*	3
Stephen Biesty's Castles, *Hooper*	15
Warfare and Weapons, *Gravett*	
Women and Girls in the Middle Ages, *Eastwood*	8
The World of the Medieval Knight, *Gravett*	17
You Wouldn't Want to Be in a Medieval Dungeon! Prisoners You'd Rather Not Meet, *MacDonald*	35, 47

Medieval Book Web

Medieval Art Arena Books

The Dragon and the Unicorn, *Cherry*	
The Duke and the Peasant, *Beckett*	
A Medieval Feast, *Aliki*	24
Pish, Posh, said Hieronymus Bosch, *Willard*	
Saint George and the Dragon, *Hodges*	
Simeon's Gift, Edwards	

Medieval Poetry Books

The Dragons Are Singing Tonight, *Prelutsky*	36
The Gargoyle on the Roof, *Prelutsky*	53

Medieval Activity Books

Knights and Castles: 50 Hands-On Activities to Experience the Middle Ages, *Hart*
Medieval Projects You Can Do, *Groves*

Fine Arts/Arts and Crafts

1. Design a town seal
2. Design a stained glass window
3. Letter in calligraphy
4. Paint a portrait of the medieval times
5. Draw a border
6. Dramatize a Robin Hood adventure
7. Finger paint paper and cut out dragon
8. Research headdresses of the time
9. Create a medieval weaving
10. Make a medieval trivia game
11. Make a musical instrument
12. Make a simple princess dress
13. Create a crown and scepter
14. Create a medieval castle painting
15. Construct a castle and take a virtual castle tour
16. Design a coat of arms
17. Create your own lance, shield, and helmet
18. Make a dragon
19. Write and perform a puppet show

Math

37. Learn about weights and measures
38. Draw a labyrinth
39. Find radius, diameter, and circumference

Science

40. Investigate the Black Plague
41. Study mythological dragons from around the world
42. Investigate falconry

Medieval Curriculum Web

Language Arts

20. Research and analyze church jobs
21. Share Arthurian legends through skits
22. Create a timeline of medieval tales
23. Research the Crusades
24. Plan a medieval feast
25. Compare Frog Prince tales
26. List rules of chivalry
27. Become a troubadour
28. Compose a slideshow presentation
29. Write a letter discussing your pet dragon's antics
30. Create question and answer flash cards
31. Devise a dragon code
32. Compare versions of *Chanticleer and the Fox*
33. Write about your personal hero
34. Write pen pal letters
35. Investigate Medieval jobs
36. Invite a poet to your school

Social Studies

43. Compare medieval knights to Samurai warriors
44. Discuss how society's rules influence people of today
45. Organize a medieval etiquette class for knights
46. Journal the life of a peasant
47. Learn about medieval crimes and punishment
48. Examine goods from each region of the world
49. Investigate the feudal system hierarchy
50. Create a life-sized knight, lord, or lady
51. Learn about King Arthur and chivalry
52. Organize outdoor games of the Middle Ages
53. Research gargoyles and take a virtual tour

2. Design a stained glass window

Arthur and the Sword, Sabuda
Arts and Literature in the Middle Ages, Cels
The Middle Ages, Corbishley
Places of Worship in the Middle Ages, Eastwood

Have students draw a simple design on white paper. Designs should have large areas of color, rather than tiny details. Place acetate over the drawn paper design, so that students can color the bars in with a black permanent marker and trace the design onto the plastic sheet. Students turn the plastic over and color the shapes in with vivid permanent markers.

3. Letter in calligraphy

Arts and Literature in the Middle Ages, Cels
Science and Technology in the Middle Ages, Findon

Have each child copy a short segment from a book. For examples and the qualifications needed to become a scribe go to Medieval Manuscripts at <www.uncp.edu/home/canada/work/markport/lit/introlit/ms.htm>.

Ink recipes may be found at Home-Made Ink Recipes at <http://members.tripod.com/~onespiritx/craft38.htm>.

Students will enjoy listening to *Vision: The Music of Hildegard Von Bingen*, as they practice calligraphy. See multimedia section for this sound recording.

4. Paint a portrait of the medieval times

Clothes and Crafts in the Middle Ages, Dawson

After students look at samples of period clothing, direct each child to paint a self-portrait in the dress of the day. Cut a frame from paper and texture with crayon rubbings.

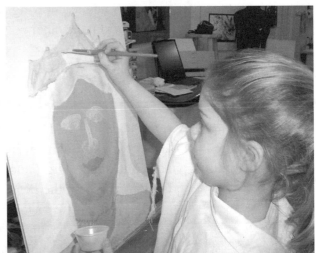

5. Draw a border

Arts and Literature in the Middle Ages, Cels
The Dragon and the Unicorn, Cherry
Life in a Medieval Monastery, Cels
Merlin and the Making of the King, Hodges
Saint George and the Dragon, Hodges

After studying a variety of borders that monks designed to decorate prayer books, design an ornate template for students to use as a guideline on parchment. Using a fine tip marker, instruct students to draw a simple design, add detailed patterns, and fill in completed designs with color.

6. Dramatize a Robin Hood Adventure

The Adventures of Robin Hood, McSpadden
The Adventures of Robin Hood, Williams

Have the class dramatize their favorite Robin Hood adventure including key characters, such as Friar Tuck and Maid Marian.

7. Finger paint paper and cut out a dragon

Behold...the Dragons!, Gibbons

Instruct students to swirl colors together on two sheets of construction paper, creating a colorful pattern and texture. The trick is to not over blend colors, because you want to see the swirls. Students cut wings from one paper and the dragon body from the other.

8. Research headdresses and head wear of the time

Clothing in the Middle Ages, Elliot
A Tournament of Knights, Lasker
Women and Girls in the Middle Ages, Eastwood

Girls make a headdress for a tournament by forming a construction paper cone shape large enough to fit

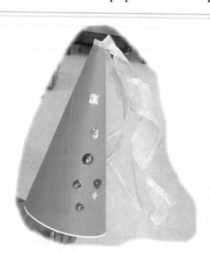

on the head. Attach a long strip of fabric to the point. Boys make a Robin Hood style hat, using brown or green construction paper. Directions for folding can be found at Parents Online <www.parents.org. uk/index.html?act_hats. htm&2>. Ribbons, jewels, or feathers may be added for a finishing touch.

9. Create a medieval weaving

Clothing in the Middle Ages, Elliot

Cut a cardboard square, the size of each weaving. Cut matching slits on opposite sides of the cardboards. Wrap yarn around cardboard through the slits. Cut one-inch wide strips of fabric for students to weave in and out of yarn, as in the example.

10. Make a medieval trivia game

Children and Games in the Middle Ages, Elliot

Make a medieval game for your library or classroom. Have students use the computer to design and print game pieces, markers, cards, and type the rules for the game. Facts and trivia for the game may be found in the unit books or at the following Medieval Games Web site. <www2.kumc.edu/itc/staff/rknight/Games.htm>.

11. Make a musical instrument

Arts and Literature in the Middle Ages, Cels
Medieval Myths, Legends, and Songs, Trembinski
Have students devise a medieval instrument, using materials found around the house. Allow time for them to demonstrate how their instrument works. Learn more about medieval music and musical instruments at The Middle Ages - Arts & Entertainment: Medieval Music <www.learner.org/exhibits/middleages/artsact.html>.

12. Make a simple princess dress

Clothes and Crafts in the Middle Ages, Dawson

Make a princess dress, based on the pattern used for costumes in the Egyptian unit. Determine the length, by doubling the child's height. Determine the width, by measure from wrist to wrist with outstretched arms. Cut a rectangle and fold the material in half lengthwise. Cut a six-inch wide and three-inch deep circle in the center, for the neckline. Use remaining material for a sash, cinching the waist up and tying in a large bow in back.

13. Create a crown and scepter

Clothes and Crafts in the Middle Ages, Dawson
A Tournament of Knights, Lasker
Have students design their own crown and scepter for a coronation. The scepter is made from a wrapping paper tube, covered with aluminum foil. Students may learn more about the scepter using this online encyclopedia: <http://en.wikipedia.org/wiki/Scepter>.

14. Create a medieval castle painting

A Medieval Castle, Bergin
Brush water across the paper immediately before the student paints stripes of yellow, red,

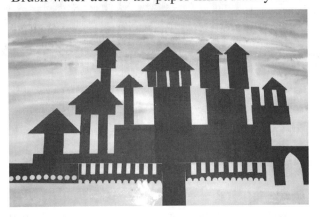

orange, or magenta across the paper, to form the sky. Water down tempera paint so the colors will run and blend together on the wet paper. Let the paper dry, before supplying the student with a variety of black construction paper pre-cut shapes from which to build a castle. Students arrange shapes and glue them to the painted sky construction paper. Have students cut additional shapes to add special accents to their castle.

15. Construct a castle and take a virtual castle tour

Castle: Medieval Days and Knights, Olmon
Knights in Shining Armor, Gibbons
A Medieval Castle, Bergin
Stephen Biesty's Castles, Hooper

Gather a variety of boxes, including round boxes such as oatmeal containers. To give the appearance of stone, students

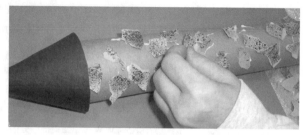

glue spattered torn paper on each box. They form the roofs from folded cardboard covered with rows of pre-cut rectangular shaped pieces of black or dark gray construction paper, giving the appearance of slate shingles. For examples of castle roofs, visit Castle Roofs <www.castles-of-britain.com/castlesd.htm>. Go to <http://kidsonthenet.com/castle/> for a virtual tour. As an extension, students could label the parts on their castle <www.castles-of-britain.com/castlesi.htm>.

16. Design a coat of arms to represent your family

Knights, Steele
Knights and Heroes, Hamilton
Knights in Shining Armor, Gibbons
Ms. Frizzle's Adventures: Medieval Castle, Cole

Learn about the history of a coat of arms at the Family Crest and Coat of Arms Web site <www.fleurdelis.com/coatofarms.htm>. See samples at <www.fleurdelis.com/samples.htm>. Learn how to make a coat of arms at <www.yourchildlearns.com/her_act.htm> or at <www.sbceo.k12.ca.us./%7Evms/carlton/page27.html>. To make a coat of arms, have students draw and color a small sample of their family crest or design to use as a pattern for the shield. Students cut their shields

from poster board and paint or use cut paper for their design.

17. Create a lance, shield, and helmet

Knights and Heroes, Hamilton
Knights in Shining Armor, Gibbons
The Medieval World, Steele
The World of the Medieval Knight, Gravett

Students may make a lance from three wrapping paper tubes taped together lengthwise

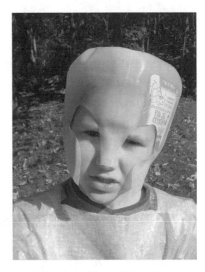

with masking tape. They then cover their lances with aluminum foil. For the hand guard, form a 14 inch decorated cone from construction paper and cut the tip off, so the cone fits tightly around the tube. To make the helmet, hold a milk jug upside down, holding on to the jug opening. Students draw a pattern onto the jug, for easier cutting. The handle will be the part covering the nose, and eyeholes will be cut from the main part of the jug. Completed helmets may be painted with silver acrylic paint.

18. Make a dragon

The Dragonology Handbook, Steer
The Knight and the Dragon, dePaola
The Loathsome Dragon, Wiesner
The Reluctant Dragon, Grahame

Form the dragon's body by wadding up and twisting newspaper into the desired shape. Masking tape helps when you use it to wrap long legs and tails. Once the dragon's basic shape is mastered, cover it with aluminum foil to add strength to the shape and to add details such as teeth and claws. Cover with small strips of paper and dip into a mixture of one part school glue and two parts water. Paint when dry.

19. Write and perform a puppet show

Good Night, Good Knight, Thomas

After reading the story *Good Night, Good Knight*, have students adapt the story for a puppet show. Puppets can be made from folded paper, as shown on the Origami Fortune Teller Craft Web site at <www.zoomschool.com/crafts/origami/fortuneteller>. Use this folded shape for the dragon's head as shown on the example. Students design and paint as many puppet characters as needed to go along with their script.

Language Arts

20. Research and analyze a list of church jobs

Life in a Medieval Monastery, Cels
Medieval Society, Eastwood

Christianity was a big part of the Middle Ages. What were the choices people had if they wanted to work within the church? Assist students in researching each job and list in a hierarchy of power order.

21. Share Arthurian legends through impromptu skits

King Arthur and the Knights of the Round Table, Williams
Tales of King Arthur: Excalibur, Talbott
Tales of King Arthur: The Sword in the Stone, Talbott

Divide students into groups and have each group read one of the Arthurian legends. Have students share legends, by performing impromptu skits. As an extension, students may write their own version of one of the Arthurian tales.

22. Create a timeline of medieval tales

Favorite Medieval Tales, Osborne

Create a timeline of medieval tales. Organize tales in chronological order from the 4th century to 1500. Discuss story forms of the times and note whether each story is a legend, ballad, or fable.

23. Research the crusades

The Medieval World, Steele
The Medieval World, Stefoff
The Middle Ages, Quigley

Have students research the "who, what, where, when, why, and how" of the crusades to gain an understanding of time and place. Have them use this information to write a paragraph summarizing what the crusades were all about. Older students might include a discussion of how the crusades influenced the Middle Ages.

24. Plan a medieval feast

A Medieval Feast, Aliki

Have students use a computer program to create a menu for a medieval feast, after a class discussion of foods from the time period. Print the menus on parchment paper. Students may use the following link for information about the food of the time period <http://library.thinkquest.org/J002390/food.html>.

25. Compare *Frog Prince* tales

Pondlarker, Gwynne

After reading *Pondlarker*, and a variety of traditional *Frog Prince* tales, have the class devise a comparison chart to use in comparing important story elements of each tale. The comparison chart may include elements such as characters, setting, plot, and illustration.

26. List rules of chivalry

The Kiss That Missed, Melling

Knights, Steele

The Medieval World, Steele

Make a list of classroom and personal rules of chivalry, starting each sentence with "Thou shalt…." Discuss whether some of the rules should be different for boys and girls. Have students look through books from this unit to find stories that are based on tales of chivalry. For examples, see <http://en.wikipedia.org/wiki/Chivalry> or <www.medieval-life.net/chivalry.htm>.

27. Become a troubadour

Medieval Myths, Legends, and Songs, Trembinski

Have the class write a poem about the Middle Ages and set it to music. Pair up students and have them travel from class to class performing their poem as a strolling minstrel. Look at the lyrics to the song, *Troubadours*, by Van Morrison at <www.harbour.sfu.ca/~hayward/van/lyrics/into.html#track4>. Read the lyrics to the class for ideas for their poems. For a definition of troubadour go to: <http://en.wikipedia.org/wiki/Troubadour>.

28. Compose a slideshow presentation

Famous People of the Middle Ages, Trembinski

Joan of Arc, Poole

Joan of Arc, Stanley

Have small groups of students choose a legendary knight or other famous person of the Middle Ages for a slideshow presentation. Include information about the person's life and why that person became famous. For a list of knights and information links, go to the Knights of the Round Table Web site <www.timelessmyths.com/arthurian/roundtable.html#List>.

29. Write a letter discussing your pet dragon's antics

Dragons, Penner

The Egg, Robertson

Ignis, Wilson

The Secret in the Matchbox, Willis

Have students write a letter to their parents apologizing for sneaking their pet dragon into school, and describing the chaos caused as a result.

30. Create question and answer flash cards

The Middle Ages, Quigley

Using index cards, and a variety of resources, have students write a question about the Middle Ages on one side of the card and the answer on the other side. These cards could be used as an assessment activity to evaluate student knowledge for this unit.

31. Devise a dragon code

Dragonology, Steer

The Dragonology Handbook, Steer

Have students devise their own dragon codes and write a letter to a classmate in that code.

Let them try to crack each other's codes. As a technology alternative, have students use a word processing program to type their letters. Then, change the font to one such as symbol or webdings, to encrypt the letter. Students put the ABC code at the bottom of the letter to help solve the encryption code.

32. Compare versions of *Chanticleer and the Fox*

Chanticleer and the Fox, Chaucer
Favorite Medieval Tales, Osborne

Compare two versions of the fable, *Chanticleer and the Fox*. Discuss similarities and differences. Have students summarize the moral of the story and apply it to present day society.

33. Write about a personal hero

Imagine You're a Knight!, Clibbon
The Kitchen Knight, Hodges
Knights and Heroes, Hamilton

Have students write about a personal hero. Compare characteristics of that hero with characteristics of heroes from medieval days. A good Web site for biographical information about people of the medieval times is the Medieval Times site at <www.schools.ash.org.au/elanorah/med.htm>.

34. Write pen pal letters describing the effect of forest's destruction

The Dragon and the Unicorn, Cherry

Have students assume the identity of the dragon or the unicorn and establish pen pal communications between the two. Have each correspond in writing about the devastation caused as a result of the king and his knights invading their peaceful habitat. Include solutions for conservation that could be applied to conservation issues today. As an extension, have students listen to "Song of the Unicorn." See the multimedia section for information about this CD.

35. Investigate medieval jobs

Archers, Alchemists, and 98 Other Medieval Jobs You Might Have Loved or Loathed, Galloway
You Wouldn't Want To Be in a Medieval Dungeon: Prisoners You'd Rather Not Meet, MacDonald

After investigating a variety of medieval jobs, have students begin their new role as assistant to the king by writing a "Help Wanted" advertisement for one of the positions. Advertisements should include a job description and necessary qualifications. Hold a medieval job fair, using visual aids, to entice applicants. As an extension, have students write a resume for a job of their choice. For more information about occupations in the Middle Ages visit Medieval Jobs at <www.castles-of-britain.com/castle32.htm> or The Worst Jobs in History at <www.channel4.com/history/microsites/W/worstjobs/medieval.html>.

36. Invite a poet to visit your school or library

"A Damsel in Distress" poem by Steve Presser

The Dragons Are Singing Tonight, Prelutsky

As a follow up to reading a selection of medieval poems, such as "Damsel in Distress" figure 2.46.1 (see page 84), invite an author, illustrator, or poet to visit your school or library to share literature and pictures of time and place.

Math

37. Learn about weights and measures

Medieval Towns, Trade, and Travel, Elliot

Discuss with students different weights and measures that were important when used to trade, barter, or purchase goods. Which of these are still used today? How are the methods the same? Have students create currency to barter or sell in exchange for classroom supplies.

38. Draw a labyrinth

Places of Worship in the Middle Ages, Eastwood

Look at some labyrinth patterns. The design repeats so the path that is walked on continues forever. Discuss why the monks used a labyrinth at the monasteries. Have students draw a labyrinth of their own.

39. Find radius, diameter, and circumference

Sir Cumference and the First Round Table, Neuschwander

Have students locate a circular item in the building or on the grounds. After discussing terms, as a class, determine the radius, diameter, and circumference of each circle.

Science

40. Investigate the Black Plague

The Medieval World, Stefoff

Read about the Black Plague or Black Death. What was it, and why was it feared? Ask students to write a report, as doctors practicing in medieval times. Include some of the potions used to control disease or cure people. Discuss cures we have today that would have ended the plague. For more information on medieval diseases and cures visit Diseases During the Middle Ages at <www.medieval-life.net/diseases.htm> and Medicine at <www. medieval-life.net/medicine.htm>. Students can try their skills as medieval doctors diagnosing patients at The Middle Ages – Health: Medieval Medicine interactive Web site <www. learner.org/exhibits/middleages/healtact2.html>.

41. Learn about mythological dragons around the world

Dragonology, Steer

The Dragonology Handbook, Steer

Dragons, Penner

Go to the Wikipedia Web site and compare physical attributes of mythical dragons. Examine Asian, European, American, and African dragons, and compile a list of physical differences such as number of heads, claws, wings, etc. Use the chart at <http://en.wikipedia.org/wiki/Dragon>.

42. Investigate falconry

Castles, Steele

A Medieval Castle, Gresko

The Medieval World, Steele

Have students research the equipment needed and the dangers involved in falconry. Why was falconry so important in the Middle Ages? For information go to Falconry Education at <www.falconry.com/educa_frm.htm> or FirstScience - Ancient Falconry at <www.firstscience.com/SITE/articles/dobney.asp>.

Social Studies

43. Compare medieval knights to samurai warriors

The Life of a Knight, Eastwood

The word Samurai means "One who serves." His job was to protect the emperor and his people. After reading about these warriors, have students compare knights and their code of ethics to samurais and their code of ethics. Use the *Knight-Samurai Comparison Chart* figure 2.46 (see page 83) to record your findings. Visit The Samurai Way @ National Geographic Magazine at <http://magma.nationalgeographic.com/ngm/0312/feature5/index.html?fs=www7.nationalgeographic.com>.

44. Discuss how society's rules influence people today

The Princess Knight, Funke

After reading this book, discuss the following questions: When Princess Violetta broke the rules of her father's expectations, what were the consequences and how did her life change? What are some of society's rules from the Middle Ages that have changed over the years? Think about your life and the expectations others have for you. What expectations do you feel need to change and what will the consequences be? How might you go about making these changes?

45. Organize an etiquette class for knights

Days of the Knights: A Tale of Castles and Battles, Maynard

A Medieval Castle, Gresko

Hold an etiquette class to prepare knights for the king's feast. Students should prepare a lesson to share with the class, based on acceptable rules of etiquette for medieval times.

46. Journal a day in the life of a peasant

Peasant, Lilly

Have students journal a day in the life of a peasant. Add details that would help the reader gain an understanding of what it was like to live in the Middle Ages.

47. Learn about medieval crimes and punishments

You Wouldn't Want to Be in a Medieval Dungeon: Prisoners You'd Rather Not Meet, MacDonald

Have small groups discuss and list common crimes and punishments of medieval times. For each, debate whether the punishment fit the crime, if the law was too harsh, or if prisoners were victims of society's beliefs at that time.

48. Examine goods from each region of the world

Medieval Towns, Trade, and Travel, Elliott

Have students investigate the Silk Route and Spice Road in the book. Trace these routes on a map. How did goods travel from one country to another? What goods did each region produce? What countries did merchants pass through selling their goods?

49. Investigate the feudal system hierarchy

Life in a Castle, Eastwood

Have groups of students investigate the feudal system hierarchy and display their findings on a poster. Posters should portray how each rung on the hierarchy affects the next. Additional information can be found at these sites: The Middle Ages: Feudal Life <www.learner.org/exhibits/middleages/feudal.html> and The Middle Ages: The Feudal System <http://library.thinkquest.org/10949/fief/hifeudal.html>.

50. Create a life-sized knight, lord, or lady

Imagine You're a Knight!, Clibbon

The Medieval World, Steele

Pair up students and have each trace around the other on large sheets of butcher-block paper. Before cutting out their bodies, have students add a cape, shield, headdress, or other accessories that a knight in armor, lord, or lady would wear. Have students cut out the image and fill in detail with paint. Students may paint in their faces or glue a digital photo of their faces on to the life-size replicas.

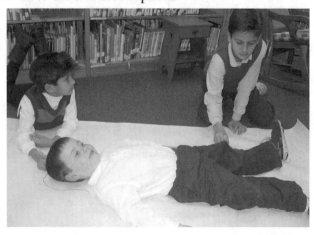 

51. Perform acts of chivalry and learn about King Arthur

The Dwarf, the Giant, and the Unicorn, Giblin

Imagine You're a Knight!, Clibbon

Tales of King Arthur: The Sword in the Stone, Talbott

What made King Arthur so great? Who was present around the Round Table? What did the knights do? Form a class of knights, to discuss and practice acts of kindness and chivalry to benefit the school or library. For more information about King Arthur, go to: <www.timelessmyths.com/arthurian/arthur.html#Arthur>. For information about the Round Table investigate this Web site: <www.timelessmyths.com/arthurian/roundtable.html>.

52. Organize outdoor games of the Middle Ages

Children and Games in the Middle Ages, Elliott

Life on a Medieval Manor, Cels

Organize stations for outdoor medieval games including walking on stilts, piggyback rides, hoops and sticks, marbles and dice, tag, leapfrog or hopscotch. Find information at Ancient and Medieval Games – History for Kids! <www.historyforkids.org/learn/games>.

53. Take a virtual tour of gargoyles

The Gargoyle on the Roof, Prelutsky

Night of the Gargoyles, Bunting

A common belief is that gargoyles were placed on buildings as protectors, keeping away evil. Take a virtual tour of gargoyles at <www.stonecarver.com/grotesque.html>, and learn more about how they were created and why. Study more about the purpose of gargoyles in the medieval churches at <http://northstargallery.com/gargoyles/aboutgargoyles.htm>. Have students create their own gargoyles from clay or play dough. Once they have dried, students may paint them gray to look like stone, and add an explanation of what their design represents.

Art Arena

The Dragon and the Unicorn, Cherry
The Duke and the Peasant, Beckett
A Medieval Feast, Aliki
Pish, Posh, Said Hieronymus Bosch, Willard
Saint George and the Dragon, Hodges
Simeon's Gift, Edwards

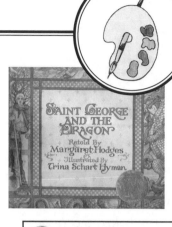

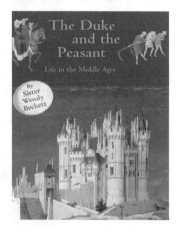

Illumination of the Medieval Times

During medieval times important documents and pages of special books, such as prayer books, were decorated with a flowered, curving designed border, known as illumination. It was called illumination because gold or silver leaf was used to make the script appear to be lit up. The gold added an element of importance to each page. The initial letter was larger and often decorated with an entire scene of the document's topic. The designs were colored with rich reds, blues, and greens, accented with stark blacks. Each design was an original work of art, even though each artist or scribe could have a signature design he was known for and the design was used several times on the manuscripts he created. *The Duke and the Peasant* is a wonderful sample of illuminated pages, containing initial letters beautifully illustrated with pictures of medieval life during each month of the calendar. *The Dragon and the Unicorn, A Medieval Feast, Saint George and the Dragon,* and *Simeon's Gift* are other

examples of books with exceptionally creative borders illuminating the text of the story. Instruct students to examine these books for examples of illumination.

Apple Tarts
(8 servings)

Ingredients:
1 unbaked piecrust

Filling:
6 golden delicious apples
½ stick butter
1 tablespoon cinnamon
2 tablespoons flour
¼ cup sugar

Glaze:
½ cup apricot jam
2 tablespoons water

Directions:
Cut peeled apples into thin slices. Arrange slices in a fan pattern on top of chilled dough. Dot with butter, and sprinkle cinnamon, sugar, and flour between layers of apples. Bake in a preheated oven at 375 degrees F for 35-45 minutes until golden. Heat jam and water in saucepan until it comes to a boil. Pour glaze over tart. Cool and serve.

Gingerbread
(12 servings)

Historical Note: In the Middle Ages, gingerbread was commonly used for soothing stomach ailments, welcoming travelers home, and many religious celebrations.

Ingredients:
½ cup shortening
3 tablespoons sugar
1 egg
1 cup dark molasses
1 cup water
2 1/3 cups flour
1 tsp. baking soda
½ tsp. salt
2 tsp. ginger
1 ½ tsp. cinnamon

Directions:
Mix shortening, sugar, and egg. Stir molasses into boiling water and add to mixture. Sift dry ingredients and add, beating until smooth. Pour into a greased and floured 9-inch pan and bake 45 minutes at 325 degrees F. Cut into 2-inch squares. Frost with cream cheese frosting.

Culminating Activities

Hold a Medieval Fair

Hold a medieval fair with all the trimmings. Play leapfrog, tug of war, three-legged races, chess, marbles, and sack races. Display the castle models, art projects, and poetry made by the class. Hold puppet shows, impromptu plays, and demonstrate juggling skills. Fill the day with demonstrations of life in medieval times, and serve fruit tarts or gingerbread. Set up booths to sell or barter goods made by merchants. Display projects done during the progression of the unit. Students wear hats, headdresses, and costumes made throughout the unit.

Medieval Assessment Rubric

Students will be able to:	Fair 1	Good 2	Mastered 3	Score
Understand the hierarchy of the feudal system				
Know the meaning of some key vocabulary: moat, allegiance, jester, and bailey				
Give examples of art styles of the Middle Ages				
Compare the lifestyles of the classes of people				
Name 3 famous knights				
Identify the years which consisted of the Middle Ages				
Know the meaning of chivalry and give examples				
Retell the story of Joan of Arc and her importance in history				
Name and label parts of a castle				
Discuss the importance of contributions of the Middle Ages				

Figure 2.55 Medieval Rubric

Multimedia Resources

Art with Joy Series: Castle [video recording]. Clearvue/eav, Inc., 1994. 32 min.
> Students draw a castle following step-by-step instructions, as they become participants in an art class. Concepts of perspective, top and bottom, near and far are emphasized, as students draw, learn facts about castles, and add original pictures to the background (Grades 1-4).

Life in the Middle Ages series [video recording] produced by Andrew Schlessinger and Tracy Mitchel. Schlessinger Media: Library Video Company, 2002. 23 min.
> Students explore medieval times through relationships among people of the time. Information includes food, clothing, housing, and entertainment of the period, depicted through historic reenactments and footage of European castles and medieval festivals (Grades 4-8).

Song of the Unicorn [sound recording] by Susan Hammond and Debra A.S. Olivia. Classical Productions for Children Ltd., 1999.
> In this musical journey through medieval times, a queen becomes ill and her children go in search of the legendary unicorn, her only chance of a cure (Grades 2-6).

Vision: The Music of Hildegard Von Bingen [sound recording]. Angel Records, 1994.
> In the 12th century, Hildegard Von Bingen wrote heavenly chants, psalms, and canticles of the Catholic Church, so unique that the "New Age Movement" embraced them (Grades 3-Adult).

Web Site Resources

Castle Xplorer <www.castlexplorer.co.uk/history.php>
> This site contains a short history of castles and information about the demise of castles and castle life.

Castles for Kids <www.castles.org/Kids_Section/Castle_Story>
> A peek inside a castle, the parts of a castle, the people of the castle, and activity ideas, such as printable coloring pages, are included.

Choose a Guide <www.mnsu.edu/emuseum/history/middleages/contents.html>
> Students learn about the Middle Ages from the perspective of a peasant, nun, knight, or merchant. They choose which one serves as their tour guide.

Knights and Armor <www.knightsandarmor.com/index.htm>
> The history of knights, information about heraldry, weapons, armor, and the life of a knight are included in this great site.

Medieval History <http://members.aol.com/TeacherNet/Medieval.html#Chiv>
> A comprehensive collection of links related to medieval times is found here.

Medieval Quest <http://library.thinkquest.org/J002390/index.html>
> This informative site, designed by students, teaches about heraldry, food, clothing, castles, and knights. Students can test their knowledge by taking an online quiz.

National Geographic's Ghosts in the Castle <www.nationalgeographic.com/castles/enter.html>
> Children explore the areas of a castle and learn about the people who lived there in this child friendly site, by National Geographic, that has a mouse as a tour guide.

ThinkQuest Virtual VR <http://library.thinkquest.org/10949/fief/hiindex.html>
> This is a very good list of topics related to the castles, knights, society, and the way people lived.

Book Resources

Fiction Books

Adventures in the Middle Ages
by Linda Bailey. Illus. Bill Slavin. Kids Can Press, 2000.
The Binkerton twins and their younger sister arrive in the midst of peasants from the Middle Ages, where Josh gets a shot at becoming a knight and the girls throw the enemy camp into total chaos, before being transported back to the Good Times Travel Agency (Grades 1-4).

The Adventures of Robin Hood
by J. Walker McSpadden. Illus. Greg Hildebrandt. Courage Books: Running Press, 2005.
Magnificent paintings and conversational text introduce readers to the legend of Robin Hood, through heroic tales of robbing the rich to give to the poor (Grades 3-6).

The Adventures of Robin Hood

by Marcia Williams. Candlewick Press, 1995.
The legend of Robin Hood is told through comic-strip drawings and irreverent humor in an enticing oversized picture book that introduces readers to Little John, Friar Tuck, Maid Marian, and more (Grades 1-4).

Arthur and the Sword

retold by Robert Sabuda. Atheneum Books for Young Readers, 1995.
When a sword buried in a steel anvil magically appears with the message that whoever is able to pull the sword from the stone will become England's next king, only Arthur is able to remove it in this retelling of an Arthurian legend illustrated with stained glass artwork (Grades K-2).

Behold…the Dragons!

by Gail Gibbons. HarperCollins, 1999.
Dragon lovers will delight in this book of dragon stories, myths and legends, and notorious dragons found throughout world literature (Grades K-3).

Chanticleer and the Fox

by Geoffrey Chaucer. Illus. Barbara Cooney. HarperCollins, 1958.
"Avoid being taken in by flattery," is the moral of this Canterbury Tale. When flattery causes Chanticleer to end up in the fox's mouth, the witty rooster escapes by demonstrating that turnabout is fair play (Grades K-2).

The Dragon and the Unicorn

by Lynne Cherry. Harcourt Brace & Company: A Gulliver Green Book, 1995.
Valerio the dragon and Allegra the unicorn are driven into hiding by a king and his knights who want to destroy the forest, slay the dragon, and capture the unicorn. Through the assistance of the king's daughter, peace is restored, and the king declares the forest and its inhabitants to be a place of love and respect (Grades K-2).

Dragonology: The Complete Book of Dragons

edited by Dugald Steer. Illus. Wayne Anderson, Douglas Carrel, and Helen Ward. Candlewick Press, 2003.
This complete book of dragons emerses the reader into dragon lore, from worldly stories of legendary dragons to dragon history, life cycle, and behavior. Bound in a leather looking cover with embedded jewels, magnificent illustrations equipped with flaps and other paper engineering techniques are sure to captivate children of all ages (Grades 2-8).

The Dragonology Handbook: A Practical Course in Dragons

edited by Dugald Steer. Candlewick Press, 2005.
In this student course in dragonology, the reader is guided through 21 lessons introduced on antiquated looking pages, containing card filled pockets (Grades 3-6).

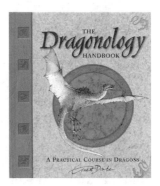

Dragons

by Lucille Recht Penner. Illus. Peter Scott. Random House, 2004.
Penner's guide for young readers relates myths about dragons from various countries and discusses their appearance and behavior (Grades K-3).

The Dwarf, the Giant, and the Unicorn: A Tale of King Arthur

retold by James Cross Giblin. Illus. Claire Ewart. Clarion Books, 1994.
When King Arthur's ship is beached on an island, he meets a dwarf, a giant, and a unicorn that help free the ship and then accompany King Arthur back to Camelot. There, the dwarf becomes the court's storyteller, the giant patrols the borders, and a special park is built for the unicorn. Ewart's vibrant watercolor paintings evoke a medieval spirit (Grades 2-5).

The Egg

by M. P. Robertson. Phyllis Fogelman Books, 2001.
When young George finds an enormous egg that hatches into a dragon, he teaches it to fly, breathe fire, rescue a damsel, and defeat a knight. Still, the dragon is lonely until he flies off and discovers a cave inhabited by other dragons like himself (Grades K-2).

Favorite Medieval Tales

by Mary Pope Osborne. Illus. Troy Howell. Scholastic Press, 1998.
This noteworthy collection of nine European medieval tales includes "The Sword in the Stone," "Robin Hood and His Merry Men," "Chanticleer and the Fox," and more (Grades 3-8).

Fighting Knights

by Rachel Wright. Illus. based on characters by Martin Handford. Candlewick Press, 2001.
As Waldo and his friends embark on their knight adventure, readers learn about knights, tournaments, and sieges (Grades K-3).

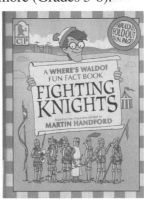

Good Night, Good Knight

by Shelley Moore Thomas. Illus. Jennifer Plecas. Dutton Children's Press, 2000.
While on night watch, the good knight hears a roar and comes to the aid of a young dragon, in need of a glass of water. Additional roars from the dragon's siblings result in several more trips for the good knight in this cumulative tale that culminates with a goodnight kiss (Grades K-2).

Ignis

by Gina Wilson. Illus. P. J. Lynch. Candlewick Press, 2001.
Even though Ignis can run faster and fly higher than his friends, it takes a trip to the top of the mountain where he finds his fire, to make him feel like a real dragon (Grades K-2).

Imagine You're a Knight!

by Meg Clibbon. Illus. Lucy Clibbon. Annick Press, 2005.
This fanciful look at a knight's life includes a look at knights in shining armor, damsels in distress, chivalry, dragons, and tournaments (Grades K-2).

Joan of Arc

by Josephine Poole. Illus. Angela Barrett. Knopf Books for Young Readers, 2005.
This picture book biography portrays a young girl who leads France to victory against the English and witnesses the crowning of King VII. Burned at the stake for heresy, years later she is canonized a saint (Grades 3-6).

Joan of Arc

by Diane Stanley. HarperTrophy, (Reprinted 2002).
Stanley's picture book biography portrays a peasant girl who at a young age hears voices of saints, leads the French army into battle against the English, is accused of being a heretic, and is burned at the stake. Five hundred years later, Joan of Arc is declared a saint (Grades 3-6).

King Arthur and the Knights of the Round Table

by Marcia Williams. Candlewick Press, 1996.
Through humorous verse and artwork rendered in comic strip format, Williams relates tales of Arthur including "Excalibur," "Morgan Le Fay," and legends of Camelot (Grades 2-6).

The Kiss That Missed

by David Melling. Barron's Educational Series, Inc., 2002.
When her busy father's good night kiss misses and escapes into the dark forest, the king's not so brave knight is sent on a journey to retrieve it. The knight catches the kiss and returns to the castle, where the princess's father promises to stop being in such a hurry (Grades K-2).

The Kitchen Knight: A Tale of King Arthur

retold by Margaret Hodges. Illus. Trina Schart Hyman. Holiday House, 1990.
In this tale from the Arthurian legends, King Arthur's nephew, Gareth, is knighted by

Lancelot. He later wages and wins a battle against the dreaded Knight of the Red Plain, rescuing the lady he has imprisoned. In doing so, he wins her love and hand in marriage (Grades K-3).

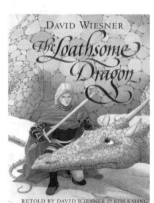

The Knight and the Dragon

by Tomie dePaola. G.P. Putnam's Sons, 1980.
When a novice knight and timid dragon duel, the outcome finds the dragon in a pool of water and the knight hung up in a tree. To the rescue comes a cookbook-laden damsel, and the knight and dragon team up to open a restaurant, in this nearly wordless book (Grades K-1).

The Loathsome Dragon

retold by David Wiesner and Kim Kahng. Illus. David Wiesner. Clarion Books, 2005.
Based on an 18th century ballad, the King of Bamborough's castle unwittingly marries an enchantress, following the death of his wife. Jealousy causes her to turn his daughter into a loathsome dragon, until her wandering brother returns and breaks the spell (Grades K-3).

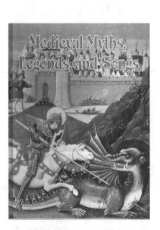

A Medieval Feast

by Aliki. HarperCollins Publishers, 1983.
Interesting facts and exquisite illustrations, based on illuminated manuscripts and Middle Age tapestries, depict the preparation needed to prepare an English manor house for a king's visit (Grades K-2).

Medieval Myths, Legends, and Songs

by Donna Trembinski. Crabtree Publishing Company, 2006.
Part of a series, this title spans storytellers, mythological gods, and tales of kings and warriors, illustrated in the likeness of an illuminated manuscript (Grades 2-5).

Merlin and the Making of the King

retold by Margaret Hodges. Illus. Trina Schart Hyman. Holiday House, 2004.
Three of Sir Thomas Mallory's *Le Morte d'Arthur* tales have been adapted and retold for younger audiences including "The Sword and the Stone," "Excalibur," and "The Lady of the Lake." Striking watercolors in regal tones include illumination (Grades 2-5).

Ms. Frizzle's Adventures: Medieval Castle

by Joanna Cole. Illus. Bruce Degen. Scholastic Press, 2003.
When Ms. Frizzle follows a student into Craig's Castle Shop, they end up in the midst of a siege of a 12th-century castle. Ms. Frizzle

and Arnold manage to save the day, before Arnold accidentally slips into the passage that takes them back to the shop (Grades K-3).

Night of the Gargoyles

by Eve Bunting. Illus. David Wiesner. Clarion Books, 1994.
Gargoyles adorning the walls of an art museum gather around a fountain at night, peeking in at mummies and suits of armor. They observe the watchman as he hurries by huddled in fear, returning to their corners of the rooftop as morning arrives (Grades 1-3).

Pish, Posh, Said Hieronymus Bosch

by Nancy Willard. Illus. Leo and Diane Dillon. Harcourt Brace Jovanovich, Publishers, 1991.
Inspired by Hieronymus Bosch's bizarre creatures, Willard's poem tells the story of a housekeeper who works for Bosch until his paintings take on a life of their own. After leaving the chaotic household, the woman discovers creatures hidden in her suitcase that convince her to return to care for them. She establishes new rules and ends up marrying Bosch (Grades 2-5).

Pondlarker

by Fred Gwynne. Simon and Schuster Books for Young Readers, 1990.
After hearing the *Frog Prince* tale, Pondlarker goes in search of a princess whose kiss might turn him into a prince. However, it isn't long before Pondlarker learns that the princess is not quite what he expects, and, so it is, he decides to remain a frog (Grades K-2).

The Princess Knight

by Cornelia Funke. Illus. Kerstin Meyer. Scholastic Inc.: The Chicken House, 2001.
After raising his daughter in the same manner as his sons, Violetta's father holds a jousting tournament, offering her hand in marriage as the prize. Disguised as a knight, the princess wins the tournament and years later marries a man of her choice, the rose gardener's son (Grades K-2).

Princess Smartypants

by Babette Cole. G.P. Putnam's Sons, 1986.
Princess Smartypants devises a variety of difficult tasks to ward off potential suitors, until she meets Prince Swashbuckle. After successfully completing several tasks, Swashbuckle implies that the princess is not so smart. She gives him a kiss that turns him into a gigantic toad and, now that she doesn't have to worry about potential suitors, the princess lives happily ever after (Grades K-2).

The Reluctant Dragon

by Kenneth Grahame. Illus. Michael Hague. Holt, Rinehart and Winston, 1983.
A Shepard boy convinces St. George not to slay the friendly sonnet-writing dragon he has befriended. The two take the boy's advice, pretend to battle one another, and St. George

convinces the townspeople that the dragon should now be quite changed (Grades K-3).

Saint George and the Dragon

by Margaret Hodges. Illus. Trina Schart Hyman. Little, Brown Young Readers, 1990.
Muted landscapes serve as quiet backdrops for this dramatic recounting of the legendary battle between Saint George and the fearsome dragon that has been spreading terror throughout the countryside. Borders depict angels, unicorns, and other creatures of medieval lore (Grades K-3).

The Secret in the Matchbox

by Val Willis. Illus. John Shelley. Farrar, Straus & Giroux, 1988.
Nobody in Bobby Bell's class wants to see what is in his secret matchbox, including Miss Potts, his teacher, who places the matchbox on her desk. "There's going to be trouble," Bobby says. Trouble there is, as the class watches the tiny dragon get bigger and bigger, until it causes so much chaos that she can no longer ignore what is happening (Grades K-2).

Simeon's Gift

by Julie Andrews Edwards and Emma Walton Hamilton. Illus. Gennady Spirin. HarperCollins Publishers, 2003.
In this exquisite book accompanied by a CD, a musician goes out into the world, hoping to find the music that lies deep within his soul. His experiences in the world lead him to discover that one can find his way if he trusts in the wonders under God's canopy (Grades 1-4).

Sir Cedric

by Roy Gerrard. Farrar Straus Giroux, 1984.
Sir Cedric goes in search of adventure and rescues Matilda from Black Ned, who has imprisoned her in a tower. When Ned returns to seek revenge, Sir Cedric convinces the townspeople to stand up to bullies. Their intervention causes Black Ned to change his ways (Grades 1-3).

Sir Cumference and the First Round Table

by Cindy Neuschwander. Illus. Wayne Geehan. Charlesbridge Publishing, 1997.
When Sir Cumference discovers that a rectangular table is not practical for meeting with other knights, he has it cut into a square, then a diamond, and so on until it forms an egg shape. Seeing a fallen tree, Lady Di suggests cutting a cross section, which solves the problem and offers a fictitious explanation for the origin of diameter, radius, and circumference (Grades K-4).

Tales of King Arthur: Excalibur

by Hudson Talbott. Books of Wonder: Morrow Junior Books, 1996.
In this third volume of *Talbott's Tales of King Arthur* series, Arthur struggles to prove himself worthy of leading his countrymen. He asks the Lady of the Lake for the noble sword,

Excalibur. Merlin advises Arthur of the scabbard's importance and Pellinore, who recognizes Arthur as a Pendragon, begs his forgiveness and joins his company (Grades 2-5).

Tales of King Arthur: The Sword in the Stone
by Hudson Talbott. Books of Wonder: Morrow Junior, 1991.
Arthur's destiny as Britain's young king is revealed when he is the only person able to draw a sword from the anvil, laying the foundation for the Arthurian tales (Grades 3-5).

A Tournament of Knights
by Joe Lasker. Thomas Y. Crowell, 1986.
As Justin prepares for his first tournament against an experienced challenger, lively drawings make readers feel they are part of this Middle Ages sporting event (Grades 1-3).

Poetry Books

The Dragons Are Singing Tonight
by Jack Prelutsky. Illus. Peter Sis. Greenwillow Books, 1993.
Included in this collection, brought to life by magnificent paintings, are poems about a lamenting dragon and a dragon that appears on a computer screen (Grades 2-6).

The Gargoyle on the Roof
by Jack Prelutsky. Illus. Peter Sis. Greenwillow Books, 1999.
Gargoyles, dragons, trolls, griffins, and other creatures of the night are the subject of this poetry anthology (Grades K-3).

Information Books

Archers, Alchemists, and 98 Other Medieval Jobs You Might Have Loved or Loathed
by Priscilla Galloway. Illus. Martha Newbigging. Annick Press, 2003.
Through tongue in cheek humor, this handbook offers detailed descriptions of lowly medieval careers, from blacksmith to illuminator. Comical illustrations add to the satire (Grades 2-6).

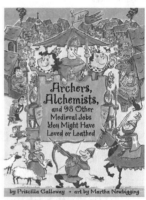

Arts and Literature in the Middle Ages
by Marc Cels. Crabtree Publishing Company, 2005.
Middle Age arts and literature come to life through period architecture, sculptures, stained glass windows, weavings, and short plays performed in towns on holy days (Grades 2-6).

Castle: Medieval Days and Knights

by Kyle Olmon. Illus. Tracy Sabin. Orchard Books: Scholastic, Inc., 2006.

Information about the Middle Ages including the castle, castle workers, knights, tournaments, and dinner at the great hall is disseminated through lively pop-ups (Grades K-4).

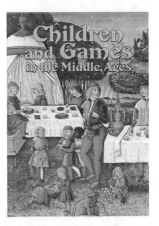

Castles

by Philip Steele. Kingfisher, 1995.

Castle life is depicted through the building of a castle, a castle town, castle defenses, castle life, and castles under attack (Grades 2-5).

Children and Games in the Middle Ages

by Lynne Elliott. Crabtree Publishing Company, 2004.

This Middle Ages title includes games, education, festivals, and more (Grades 2-4).

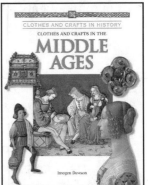

Clothes and Crafts in the Middle Ages

by Imogen Dawson. Gareth Stevens Publishing, 2000.

Tapestries, illuminated manuscripts, heraldry, pilgrimages, and minstrels are a few of the subjects included to inform the reader about Middle Age clothing and crafts. Craft activities follow the informational section (Grades 2-6).

Clothing in the Middle Ages

by Lynne Elliot. Crabtree Publishing Company, 2004.

The process of making cloth from fibers, fur from animal skins, and wool are detailed, followed by descriptions of the different styles of clothing worn in the Middle Ages (Grades 3-6).

Days of the Knights: A Tale of Castles and Battles

by Christopher Maynard. DK Publishing, Inc., 1998.

Medieval battles, fairs, knight school, tournaments, royal visits, and castles are all part of the fare in these Eyewitness Readers (Grades 2-4).

Famous People of the Middle Ages

by Donna Trembinski. Crabtree Publishing Company, 2006.
Powerful kings, women rulers, heroic peasants, explorers, and criminals are part of the mix in this introduction to notorious medieval persons (Grades 2-5).

Food and Feasts in the Middle Ages

by Lynne Elliott. Crabtree Publishing Company, 2004.
A variety of foods and how they were preserved, seasoned, prepared, and presented as works of art give children an accurate picture of foods and society during the Middle Ages (Grades 2-4).

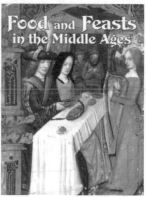

In the Time of Knights

by Shelley Tanaka. Illus. Greg Ruhl. Hyperion Books for Children, 2000.
The age of chivalry is brought to life through a tale of William Marshall who, at 13, was sent to a castle in Normandy to learn to be a knight. He fought bravely in combat and went on to joust in tournaments throughout France and England, winning many victories (Grades 3-7).

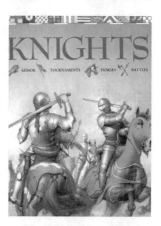

Knights

by Philip Steele. Kingfisher Publications, 1998.
From the knight's code to the end of chivalry every aspect of knighthood is covered, including biographical sketches of notorious knights and tales of knights found in fiction (Grades 2-6).

Knights and Heroes

by John Hamilton. ABDO Publishing Company, 2006.
Part of the Fantasy and Folklore series, this book includes information about becoming a knight, battle tactics, tournaments, and jousting. There is also a section about King Arthur (Grades 3-6).

Knights in Shining Armor

by Gail Gibbons. Little, Brown & Company, 1995.
Gibbons discusses the Middle Ages, describes the life of a knight, and provides information about legendary knights, such as King Arthur and Sir Lancelot (Grades K-3).

Life in a Castle

by Kay Eastwood. Crabtree Publishing Company, 2004.
Various types of castles, their construction, and what it was like to be part of the castle life is the focus of this book that includes a section on forts of the world (Grades K-6).

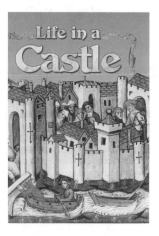

Life in a Medieval Monastery

by Marc Cels. Crabtree Publishing Company, 2005.
Life in a Medieval Monastery covers religion, monks and nuns, centers of study, responsibilities in a monastery, and noteworthy monasteries (Grades 2-6).

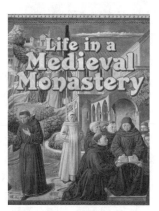

The Life of a Knight

by Kay Eastwood. Crabtree Publishing Company, 2004.
Armor, weapons, heraldry, tournaments, and chivalry span the content of this book, illustrated with exquisite borders against a parchment looking backdrop (Grades 2-6).

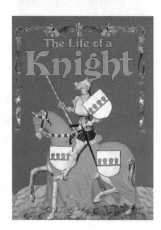

Life on a Medieval Manor

by Marc Cels. Crabtree Publishing Company, 2005.
From peasants to lords and ladies, this title shows what it was like to be part of the community living on a manor during medieval times (Grades 2-6).

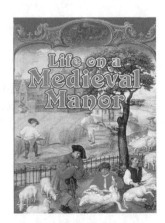

A Medieval Castle

by Marcia S. Gresko. Gale: Thomson Press, 2003.
Gresko's book describes the workings of a medieval castle including noble strongholds, the castle community, amusements, and the castle at war (Grades 2-4).

A Medieval Castle: The Inside Story of a Castle and Its Inhabitants

by Mark Bergin. Peter Bedrick Books, 2001.
Designing, building, and caring for a castle tell the story of a castle and its inhabitants, depicted in cross-sectioned illustrations (Grades 2-6).

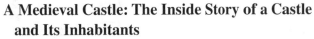

Medieval Muck

by Mary Dobson. Oxford University Press, 1998.
This behind the scenes look at medieval life captures the dark side of the times with a look at dungeons, pollution, punishments, and difficult jobs (Grades 2-6).

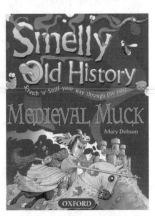

Medieval Society

by Kay Eastwood. Crabtree Publishing Company, 2004.
Kings and queens, lords and ladies, knights, peasants, and townspeople are depicted within their settings, offering a glimpse into the medieval period (Grades 2-6).

Medieval Towns, Trade, and Travel

by Lynne Elliott. Crabtree Publishing Company, 2004.
Castle conveniences, pollution solutions, punishment tactics, and plagues are just a few of the topics dealt with in a humorous manner (Grades 2-6).

The Medieval World

by Philip Steele. Kingfisher, 2000.
Knighthood, homes, castle life, fortresses, battle, and the end of a time period are addressed incorporating maps, diagrams, and delightful illustrations (Grades 2-8).

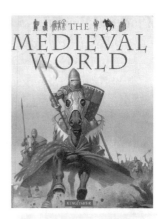

The Medieval World

by Rebecca Stefoff. Marshall Cavendish Corporation: Benchmark Books, 2005.
The rise of European states, conquering powers, the Black Death, peasant risings, and the growth of cities, offer readers an understanding of the medieval world (Grades 3-6).

The Middle Ages

by Mike Corbishley. Facts on File, Inc., 2003.
The Middle Ages period unfolds through documents and artwork that reconstruct life of the period. Empires that defined the ancient world and the historical significance of individual countries that make up Europe are examined (Grades 3-8).

The Middle Ages

by Mary Quigley. Heinemann Library, 2003.
This discussion of medieval life and times gives an overview of culture and society (Grades 3-6).

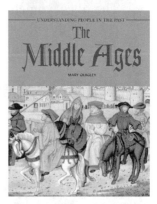

Peasant

by Melinda Lilly. Illus. Cheryl Goettemoeller. Rourke Publishing LLC, 2003.
The daily life of men, women, and children are depicted in this introduction to the work and lifestyle of a peasant living in Europe during the Middle Ages (Grades K-3).

Places of Worship in the Middle Ages

by Kay Eastwood. Crabtree Publishing Company, 2004.
The importance of the Church and daily life is the focus of this book that includes pilgrimages, Christian art, cathedrals, Judaism, mosques, crusaders, and world religion (Grades 2-6).

Science and Technology in the Middle Ages

by Joanne Findon and Marsha Groves. Crabtree Publishing Company, 2005.
Inventions and how they affected life during the Middle Ages are shown in relation to areas such as farming, medicine, and timekeeping (Grades 2-6).

Stephen Biesty's Castles

by Meredith Hooper. Enchanted Lion Books, 2004.
Stories about 10 real castles that can actually be visited, the kings who had them built, and their inspiration for building a castle are related in this oversized book (Grades 2-6).

Warfare and Weapons

by Christopher Gravett. Smart Apple Media, 2005.
Readers are drawn into the Middle Ages through descriptions of arms and armor, sieges, horses, and weapons (Grades 3-5).

Women and Girls in the Middle Ages

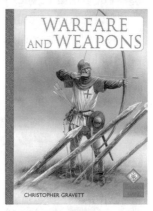

by Kay Eastwood. Crabtree Publishing Company, 2004.
The roles women in society played during the Middle Ages are detailed through discussions of family, church, women's rights, and powerful women of the period (Grades 2-6).

The World of the Medieval Knight

by Christopher Gravett. Illus. Brett Breckon. Peter Bedrick Books, 1996.
From castle life to training for knighthood, including armor, weaponry, jousting, and chivalry, this book takes a comprehensive look at the world of knighthood (Grades 3-6).

You Wouldn't Want to Be in a Medieval Dungeon: Prisoners You'd Rather Not Meet

by Fiona MacDonald. Illus. David Antram. Franklin Watts, 2003
Would you want to work in a medieval jail, upon your return home from fighting wars in far-away countries? This look at prison conditions and lifestyle may convince you that this is not exactly the type of job you had in mind (Grades 2-6).

Activity Books

The Duke and the Peasant: Life in the Middle Ages

by Sister Wendy Beckett. Illus. with Duc de Berry's Tres Riches Heures. Prestel-Verlag, 1997.
Part of the Adventures in Art series, this richly illustrated book of hours follows the daily lives of medieval peasants and nobles month by month through the seasons (Grades 2-5).

Knights and Castles: 50 Hands-On Activities to Experience the Middle Ages

by Avery Hart and Paul Mantell. Williamson Publishing, 1998.
Instructions for building a castle, playing games like Bocci, and creating stained glass windows help children experience what it was like to live in the Middle Ages (Grades 3-6).

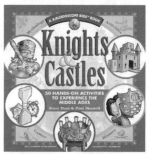

Medieval Projects You Can Do

by Marsha Groves. Crabtree Publishing Company, 2006.
Medieval dress, homes, and food are discussed, followed by a related project, such as building a trebuchet or participating in a medieval feast (Grades 2-6).

Name _____

Peacock (Peafowl) Internet Research

Find out the following information about peacocks. Use these Web sites to find the answers.
http://www.rollinghillswildlife.com/animals/p/peafowl/
http://members.aol.com/Cryptic4/index.html

The male peafowl is called the _____ and the female peafowl is called the _____
_____.

What is their size? _____
_____

List some characteristics: _____
_____

Describe their coloring: _____
_____

What is their lifespan? _____
_____

What does their diet consist of? _____
_____

Describe their habitat and where they originated: _____
_____
_____

What are a few interesting facts? _____
_____
_____
_____

Figure 2.19 Peacock Internet Research

Comparing Knights and Samurai Warriors

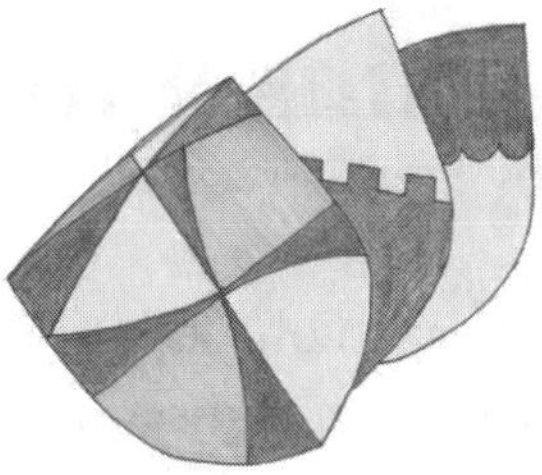

Name _____

Write yes or no beside each item under the Knight and Samurai Warriors column. Use medieval books and this Web site for help determining your answer.

http://magma.nationalgeographic.com/ngm/0312/feature5/index.html?fs=www7.nationalgeographic.com

Knights		Samurai Warriors
	Wore Armor	
	Attacked on horseback	
	Fought with swords and lances	
	Besieged castles (protected and attacked)	
	Lived by code of honor	
	Their name means "one who serves"	
	Considered an honored position	
	Loyal to an emperor	
	Loyal to a king or queen	

Figure 2.46 Knight–Samurai Comparison Chart

From *Curriculum Connections for Tree House Travelers for Grades K-4* by Jane Berner, Sabrina Minser, and Helen Burkart Presser. Columbus, OH: Linworth Publishing, Inc. Further reproduction prohibited. Copyright © 2008.

Damsel in Distress

by Steve Presser

I headed off with my valiant horse
To save a damsel in distress.
We rode for three long days and nights
In search of the dragon's address.
The fiery beast was sitting down
Sipping a cup of herbal tea,
When the damsel shrieked, "Save me now!
Whatever has taken thee?"
The dragon groaned, "Oh knight, kind sir,
Can you please take her far from here?
I've kept her captive for countless days
All she does is scream in my ear!"
The herbal tea looked good to me,
And the dragon seemed pretty swell,
I asked to stay, the dragon obliged,
And we bid the damsel farewell.

Figure 2.46.1 Damsel in Distress

UNIT 3
Destination Ancient Egypt

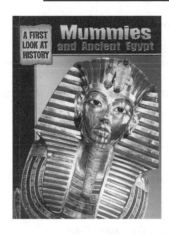

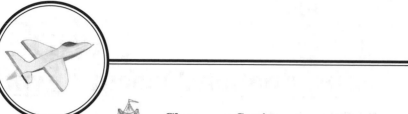

Travel Itinerary

Classroom Setting

Classroom Setting Supplies

- small table
- columns
- sheet
- large plastic jars
- crockery water jars
- books on ancient Egypt
- wooden bowls and spoons
- paper palm trees made by students

Word Wall

pyramid	Nile River
amulet	Book of the Dead
scarab	Sphinx
mummy	sarcophagus
pharaoh	Ba and Ka
hieroglyphics	papyrus
shabtis	mastabas
Sahara Desert	

Magic Tree House Book Annotations

Mummies in the Morning

by Mary Pope Osborne. Illus. Sal Murdocca. Random House, 1993.
Jack and Annie's magic tree house takes them to ancient Egypt where they follow a black cat into a pyramid. There, they encounter Hutepi, a ghost-queen who needs their help finding her Book of the Dead so that she may get through the Underworld. Only then will she be able to journey on to the Next Life. After returning the scroll and a scepter to the mummy, Jack and Annie get lost in false passages until they are led to safety by the mysterious black cat (Grades K-3).

Mummies and Pyramids

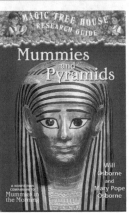

by Will Osborne and Mary Pope Osborne. Illus. Sal Murdocca. Random House, 2001.
Through illustrations, photographs, and fascinating text, this non-fiction companion to *Mummies in the Morning* offers an overview of ancient Egypt including everyday life, gods and goddesses, mummies, funerals, pyramids, and tomb treasures. There is also a special section on King Tut (Grades K-4).

Mummies in the Morning Critical Thinking Questions

1. Propose an alternative title for this book and tell how you decided upon that title.
2. If you could take Jack or Annie's place, what choices would you make differently?
3. How might the plot have changed if Jack and Annie had some prior knowledge of ancient Egypt? How would this have changed their journey?
4. Based on the outcome of other places Jack and Annie have visited, what prediction could you make about the outcome if they were placed in another risky position?
5. Compile a list of character traits that Jack and Annie displayed during their adventure to ancient Egypt.

Mummies in the Morning Curriculum Connections

1. Keep a journal of facts

Have students keep a journal of vocabulary words and facts discovered by Jack and Annie while in the time of the ancient Egyptians. Note the time period, place, events, and vocabulary.

2. Crack the code

Jack and Annie had to help the queen crack the code. Have students write their own hieroglyphic messages to trade with their classmates. Visit the Egyptian Name Translator at <www.eyelid.co.uk/e-name.htm> to create individual codes. This site translates each letter the student types into hieroglyphics. Have a class master key of the symbols to aid in cracking the codes.

3. Learn about mirages

Jack and Annie thought the ghosts were just a mirage. What is a mirage? Do mirages really happen? Visit <http://en.wikipedia.org/wiki/Mirage> to view photos and learn about this real phenomenon.

4. Follow the Nile

Hutepi was called the Queen of the Nile. What is the Nile and where is it located? Have students follow the route of the Nile River on a map of Egypt. View the maps and fact file at The Nile River site <www.mbarron.net/Nile/>. Have students list the countries through which the Nile flows.

5. Create a funeral procession shoebox diorama

Have students create shoebox dioramas, depicting a scene from the Egyptian funeral procession that Jack and Annie saw upon arriving in ancient Egypt. Have students pull their dioramas in a procession.

6. Compare Magic Tree House settings

Compare and contrast the setting for the tree house at both locations, Frog Creek and ancient Egypt. How was the landscape different? Compare the two types of tree house trees. Use a Venn diagram to record findings. Have students divide into groups and construct one of the scenes using paper, paint, and cardboard.

7. Make a souvenir bookmark of Egyptian travels

Using a computer-drawing program, have students make a souvenir bookmark of their travels to Egypt. Include a drawing of a favorite scene or character from the story.

8. Act out a scene from the book

Have students perform a skit recreating a favorite scene from the book. Use props and costumes.

9. Journal Magic Tree House "M" clues

Some Magic Tree House books have clues about the mysterious "M." Have students keep a journal of the clues found. Clues can be added as additional Magic Tree House books are read.

Mummies and Pyramids Curriculum Connections

1. Collect and compare soil samples

After reading about the different kinds of soil that could be found in ancient Egypt, have students collect soil samples from around home and school. Are the samples red land, black land, or clay? Discuss potential uses for different types of soil.

2. Create a sedimentary tube

Locate a clear tube that can be sealed on both ends. Put one cup of three or more different kinds of soil in the tube. Fill the tube with water and seal the top. Shake until all soil samples are well mixed. Set the tube in an isolated place, where it will not be bumped or disturbed. Later, examine the tube without moving it. The heavier soils should fall to the bottom.

3. Become a crafter

After reading the list describing craft people, have students choose the craft for which they are best suited. Have them draw plans or actually create an object for the crafter they chose. Their designs should reflect ancient Egypt style. Have students create plans or an object that could be used in modern day Egypt. Compare modern plans or objects with traditional ones such as boats. Compare the tools and materials used. Discuss the usefulness of each item.

4. Tell about your Ba and Ka

Ancient Egyptians believed that every living person's body held a Ba and a Ka. *Mummies and Pyramids* discusses how they believed that a person's Ka was their life force and an individual's talents and likes were part of their Ba. Have students write about their Ba and how they are unique.

5. Draw a map of Egypt

Draw a map of Egypt that includes rivers, cities, and deserts. Mark the locations where some important artifacts have been found along with where the Mastabas and the pyramids are located. List the treasures that have been found at each location.

6. Create a shabtis figure

Ask each student to bring in a small plastic bottle, such as a juice bottle. Wrap newspaper around the top of the bottle and tape it on to form a shape. Once a simple smooth shape

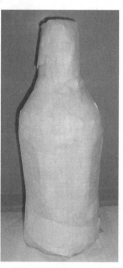

is attained, cover the bottle with papier-mâché. Mix equal parts school glue and water to dip small strips of newsprint paper into before layering around the bottle. Dry completely. Draw a shabtis figure onto the bottle and color it with permanent markers or paint.

7. Research an Egyptologist

After discussing the dangers involved in being an Egyptologist and listing the tools they need for work, have students research Howard Carter. Record findings in a report.

8. Compare your lifestyle with the ancient Egyptian lifestyle

Have one group compile a list of items they would have found in an ancient Egyptian home. Have another group compile a list of items found in their own homes. Compare items on a large Venn diagram. Discuss how these items reflected the lifestyle of each household.

Ancient Egypt Fiction Books

Ancient Egypt Art Arena: Biographies of King Tut

Ancient Egypt Book Web

Ancient Egypt Activity Books

Ancient Egypt Information Books

Fine Arts/Arts and Crafts

1. Decorate an entrance with hieroglyphics
2. Sculpt a 3-D plaster wall plaque
3. Design placemats for the pharaoh's dinner party
4. Make a sarcophagus
5. Produce a vermiculite and plaster carving
6. Create the Egyptian queen's beads
7. Make an amulet for an Egyptian necklace
8. Do a choral reading of "The Mummy's Curse"
9. Create paper pyramids
10. Listen to a song from the opera, *Aida*

Science

24. Discover how to use rods to move a box
25. Mummify a piece of fruit
26. Build an Egyptian shaduf
27. Design and create an invention

Ancient Egypt Curriculum Web

Language Arts

11. Compare creation myths
12. Create a timeline of the fall of Egypt
13. Make a Book of the Dead
14. Create a cartouche
15. Write your own verse-in-rhyme
16. Compare *The Egyptian Cinderella* to other versions of Cinderella
17. Create an Egyptian scrapbook
18. Broadcast ancient Egyptian news
19. Share mummy riddles
20. Retell a legend in story strip format
21. Set an adventure in ancient Egypt

Social Studies

28. Learn what kind of jobs an archaeological dig entails
29. Sample Egyptian cuisine
30. Create a scene from ancient Egyptian life
31. Design the top for a canopic jar
32. Investigate jobs involved in working for the pharaoh
33. Design an Egyptian warrior shield
34. Portray Egyptian gods and goddesses
35. Make a list of quarry tasks
36. Plan a trip to ancient Egypt
37. Map out Tutankhamen's exhibit route
38. Create a character web about Hatshepsut
39. Explore the pyramids

Math

22. Calculate the cost of bartered goods
23. Create an Egyptian wall border

STATION ROTATIONS - Set up stations throughout the unit to accommodate differentiated learning.

Station 1: *Fine Arts* - While listening to *Aida: Triumphal Choruses and March*, paint a free-style picture conveying how the music makes you feel. Describe those feelings on an index card to accompany your painting. #10

Station 2: *Math* - Use symmetry and tessellation to design an Egyptian wall border. #23

Station 3: *Language Arts* - Write a script to use in broadcasting ancient Egypt news. Practice reading the script in preparation for a broadcast to the class. #18

Station 4: *Science* - Mummify a piece of fruit. Display mummified fruit and keep an observation log of its appearance over a period of time. #25

Curriculum Connections

Fine Arts/Arts and Crafts

1. Decorate an entrance with hieroglyphics

Egypt in Spectacular Cross-Section, Ross
Have each student assume the role of novice artist, master artist, or color artist. The novice artists draw the hieroglyphics on the entrance in red ink. The master artists check their work, and they trace over the lines in black. The color artists add color to all of the designs inscribed on the wall. After decorating the entrance with hieroglyphics, have artists share how each felt about their participation in the artwork. Could they do that same job for a lifetime? Record comments and discuss results.

2. Sculpt a 3-D plaster wall plaque

Curse of the Pharaohs: My Adventures with Mummies, Hawass
Have students roll out a slab of modeling clay until it is thick enough to be able to be carved into deeply. Draw a pencil pattern of an Egyptian design. Place the pattern on top of the clay slab. Trace over the design so the design is etched into the surface of the clay. Remove the pattern, so students can begin to carve deeply into the modeling clay, creating different depths in the clay. After the entire design is carved, build a clay wall around the edge of the clay slab, pressing in tightly onto the slab, so that when the plaster is poured

onto the carved design, it will not leak. Pour plaster, allowing it to set up overnight. Carefully, remove clay from the plaster. If a corner should break, it only adds to the charm of the ancient Egyptian wall plaque. While working on their carvings, students may listen to a sound recording of ancient Egyptian stories. See *Egyptian Treasures: Mummies and Myths* sound recording in multimedia section.

3. Design placemats for the Pharaoh's dinner party

100 Things You Should Know About Ancient Egypt, Walker
After looking at the many designs and patterns, have students design a pattern for a placemat. Using construction paper, pre-cut many different geometric shapes of different colors and sizes. Have students begin with a basic stripe or simple design. Then build on top of it, layer by layer with colors and shapes, until they have built an ornate pattern.

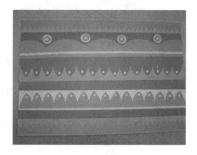

4. Make a sarcophagus

The Amazing Pop-Up Pull-Out Mummy, Hawcock
Egyptian Mummies, McCall
Egyptian Mummies, Pemberton
Have students draw the top of a sarcophagus in the likeness of King Tut on a large piece of cardboard. Paint it with royal blue paint and use gold glitter for the horizontal stripes. Cut out the design and tape a six-inch strip of cardboard around the edge to make it appear three-dimensional, like the sides of a box. Paint and glitter stripes on the sides or decorate with hieroglyphics.

5. Produce a vermiculite and plaster carving

Zekmet, the Stone Carver, Stolz
Students experience what Zekmet felt like when he was commissioned to carve a stone

for the Pharaoh. Mix equal parts vermiculite and water. Pour mixture into an 8 oz. milk carton for each student.

Allow mixture to sit overnight. Carefully tear the paper carton from around the set plaster. Have students use clay-carving tools to carve into the block, cutting away small pieces at a time and gradually cutting deeper. Simple designs work best. Dry completely. Coat with polyurethane to preserve the sculpture.

6. Create the Egyptian queen's beads

Hatshepsut, His Majesty, Herself, Andronik

Cut several triangles from ornate wallpaper, ½ inch wide at the top 2 inches on each side, coming to a point on the bottom, so the triangle is narrow and long. Place a small strip of glue on the back of the triangle down the middle. Beginning on the ½ inch wide side of

 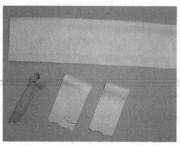 

the triangle, lay the straw across the top and roll the straw down to the point of the triangle. Dry in place on the straw. Once the beads are dry, cut the straw into pieces, close to the edge of each bead so the straw doesn't show on either side, and string them to make beads, fit for a queen.

7. Make an amulet for an Egyptian necklace

Mummies, Pyramids, and Pharaohs, Gibbons

An amulet was a symbol of something that was very important to the Egyptians and their way of life. Many of their designs were symbols of their gods or what their gods did. Ask students what is important in their culture and then have them design an amulet. To make an amulet for the center of a necklace, carve deeply into clay and pour plaster into the carved design. Once it is dry, glue it onto one of the center papers of a necklace, like the one you made for the queen's beads. Follow up with a discussion of the significance of each design.

8. Do a choral reading of "The Mummy's Curse"

After reading Steve Presser's poem, divide students into two groups. Have each group alternate reading verses, until the final verse, which is read together, creating a choral affect. See figure 3.45 "The Mummy's Curse" on page 120.

9. Create paper pyramids

Egypt in Spectacular Cross-Section, Ross
Mummies and Ancient Egypt, Ganeri
Pyramids, Hyman
Pyramids & Mummies, Simon

Cut 3 six-foot tall triangle shapes. Mix up sand-colored tempera paint and supply students with 3 inch x 6 inch rectangular shaped foam stamps. Instruct them to stamp the blocks in even rows, beginning at the bottom and working their way to the top. The point of the pyramid can be covered with gold glitter twelve inches from the top.

10. Listen to a song from the opera, *Aida*

Aida, Price

Discuss and retell the storyline of Aida and how the opera served as inspiration for writing the book. What are the similarities and differences between an opera and a play? Listen to "Aida: Triumphal Choruses and March," song number ten on *Pavarotti's Opera Made Easy: My Favourite Opera for Children*. Replay the opera song after hearing the story (Grades 1-3).

Language Arts

11. Compare creation myths

The Star Bearer: A Creation Myth from Ancient Egypt, Hofmeyr

Have students compare *The Star Bearer* creation myth to creation myths from other countries found in Virginia Hamilton's *In the Beginning: Creation Stories from Around the World*. Use a comparison chart to compare title, author, illustrations, characters, setting, storyline, outcome, and country.

12. Create a timeline depicting events that led to the decline of the Egyptian Empire

Egypt, Steele

Have students create a timeline of events that led to the fall of the Egyptian Empire, and the fall of the time of the pharaohs ruling Egypt. Discuss what happened after the fall of Egypt and who ruled Egypt until it became part of Rome.

13. Make a Book of the Dead

Gods and Goddesses in the Daily Life of the Ancient Egyptians, McCall

Mummies Unwrapped!, Weinberger

After reading about the symbols of the gods of ancient Egypt and studying the illustrations, create a group Book of the Dead. Use matte board for the cover and construction paper for the pages. Cut matte board ½ inch larger than the paper size you plan to use. Score front and back of the cover ½ inch from the side where the spine of the book will be, to allow the cover to open easily. Line up cover with pages and punch holes. Lace the book together. Decorate with jewels and glitter, or with cut paper designs. Represent a different god of the Egyptian world and information on each page. There are more than 1000 gods to represent.

14. Create a cartouche

The 5,000-Year-Old Puzzle: Solving a Mystery of Ancient Egypt, Logan
Ancient Egypt, Malam
Writing in Ancient Egypt, Fine
After looking at the project books, have students go to Virtual-Egypt: The Egyptian People's Papyrus at <www.Virtual-Egypt.com> to find hieroglyphics matching the alphabet. Have students write their names in hieroglyphics. After placing all of the names in a bag, take turns drawing one to decode.

15. Write your own verse in rhyme

Croco'nile, Gerrard
Have students write verse in rhyme about different aspects of Egyptian life and read their writings in class. Compile poems in a book.

16. Compare *The Egyptian Cinderella* to other versions of *Cinderella*

The Egyptian Cinderella, Climo

There are over 500 versions of *Cinderella*. Compare the Egyptian version to a traditional version of *Cinderella* and one of the ethnic versions such as *The Persian Cinderella*, *Moss Gown*, or *Yeh Shen*. Comparisons should include characters, setting, plot, conflict, and outcome. As an extension, have students reenact different versions of *Cinderella* through impromptu skits.

17. Create an Egyptian scrapbook

The 5,000-Year-Old Puzzle: Solving a Mystery of Ancient Egypt, Logan
Students will enjoy creating a scrapbook-style journal of facts and pictures they gather about ancient Egypt. Have students write letters and postcards to one another to save in their journals. They may also design their own scrapbook covers.

18. Broadcast ancient Egyptian news

The Egyptian News: The Greatest Newspaper in Civilization, Steedman
After reading about Egyptian news, brainstorm topics to assign to half the class to use in writing a broadcast. Allow the other half to use those completed reports to broadcast the news. Broadcasters should dress as ancient Egyptians to be videotaped for a presentation to share with others.

19. Share mummy riddles with your friends

Mummy Riddles, Hall
Fold an 8-1/2 inch x 11 inch piece of construction paper in half horizontally. Have students write and illustrate the riddle on the front and the answer inside. Display so students can read the questions, and check their answers by lifting the flap.

20. Retell a legend in a story strip

Ghosts of the Nile, Harness

Gift of the Nile: An Ancient Egyptian Legend, Mike

Discuss the meaning of legend. Have each student retell the legend in a story strip. Be sure to include a beginning, middle, end, and all of the key points. Exchange story strips and have students retell one another's story.

21. Set an adventure in ancient Egypt

Bill and Pete Go Down the Nile, dePaola

I Am the Mummy Heb-Nefert, Bunting

I, Crocodile, Marcellino

Nefertari: Princess of Egypt, Angeletti

Zoom Upstream, Wynne-Jones

Share each of these stories with a group of students. Discuss each story's setting and the importance of the setting to the story. Have students make up their own adventures, setting them in ancient Egypt.

Math

22. Calculate the cost of bartered goods

100 Things You Should Know About Ancient Egypt, Walker

1001 Facts About Ancient Egypt, Steedman

Ancient Egyptians often bartered for goods they needed. Build a simple scale and use a standard unit of measurement to weigh different items in the classroom. After assigning a cost to each unit of measurement, have students weigh items and calculate their cost.

23. Create an Egyptian wall border

Clothes and Crafts in Ancient Egypt, Balkwill

Have students begin with a simple design of bright colors with a three-color pattern that will repeat about every foot. Cut out shapes and place them on the strip of paper, before gluing, to allow students to adjust sizes and decide how often the patterns will repeat. This is an excellent activity for teaching symmetry and tessellation. Make sure to showcase completed artwork.

Science

24. Discover how to use rods to move a box

Who Built the Pyramid?, Hooper

After investigating the tasks available to workers in a stone quarry, supply students with a box large enough to fit a student sitting down. Also needed are 8 one-inch dowel rods, or sturdy cardboard tubes, all the same size and longer than the box is wide. Allow students to experiment with placing the rods under the box to make the box roll, until they can move a student across the room. As the box moves forward, have students take the rods from behind the box and place them under the front to allow the box to continue moving.

25. Mummify a piece of fruit
Cat Mummies, Trumble
Mummies Made in Egypt, Aliki
Tutankhamun: The Boy King, Gaff
After reading about the process of mummification in ancient Egypt, have each student mummify a piece of fruit. Learn how at <http://www.neferchichi.com/fruitystep1.html>.

26. Build an Egyptian shaduf
100 Things You Should Know About Ancient Egypt, Walker
Mummies and Ancient Egypt, Ganeri
After looking at a model shaduf, have students build their own. Study how it works and evaluate how you could use this tool to help lift heavy objects. How could a tool such as this help in your daily life?

27. Design and create an invention
Ghosts of the Nile, Harness
Look What Came from Egypt, Harvey
After researching Egyptian inventions, have students tell how they helped improve life then and now. Have each student design and create an invention to share.

Social Studies

28. Learn what kind of jobs an archaeological dig entails
Egypt, Steele
Egyptology, Ikram
Egyptology: Search for the Tomb of Osiris, Steer
List the jobs involved in going on an archaeological expedition. Debate which of the jobs would be the most interesting. Have students discuss which they would like to do and why.

29. Sample Egyptian cuisine
Ghosts of the Nile, Harness
Gather Egyptian recipes available at Tour Egypt! <www.touregypt.net/recipes> and have each student select one to make and share with the class. For a simpler sampling, have a taste testing party with figs, dates, pomegranates, grapefruits, raisins, papayas, and other foods associated with ancient Egypt. Determine which food was most popular, by recording favorites on a simple bar graph.

30. Create a scene from ancient Egyptian life

Mummies and Ancient Egypt, Ganeri
Provide students with wooden blocks to create a
3-D scene from ancient Egyptian life. Have students discuss everyday life in ancient Egypt.

31. Design the tops for canopic jars

You Wouldn't Want to Be an Egyptian Mummy! Disgusting Things You'd Rather Not Know, Stewart
Have students paint and design an oatmeal box
for the top of a canopic jar. Wrap the lids with designs on construction paper of Imsety,
Hapy, Duamutef or Qebehsenuef. Enlarge thumbnail examples as needed to correspond to
containers used. Once the design is
completed and the paper is folded,
glue the bottom edge onto the jar
lid edge so the design stands up for
viewing.

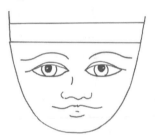

32. Investigate jobs involved in working for the pharaoh

Mummies, Pyramids, and Pharaohs: A Book About Ancient Egypt, Gibbons
Make a list of jobs available under the pharaoh and describe each one. Have students select a job they would like and tell why.

33. Design an Egyptian warrior shield

Going to War in Ancient Egypt, Millard
Warriors decorated their shields with colors and symbols that
represented what was important in their lives. Allow students
to design their own shields, depicting what is important to
them.

34. Portray Egyptian gods and goddesses

Gods and Goddesses in the Daily Life of the Ancient Egyptians, McCall
Nefertari: Princess of Egypt, Angeletti
Have students portray an Egyptian god or goddess by designing
their own costumes and becoming that character for a day.

35. Make a list of quarry tasks

Egypt in Spectacular Cross-Section, Ross

Who Built the Pyramid?, Hooper

Organize a list of jobs ancient Egyptians did in a stone quarry. Have students imagine working there and predict special skills needed to complete different tasks in the quarry. Discuss problems that workers may encounter in any given job that the overseer may give them.

36. Plan a trip to Egypt

Adventures in Ancient Egypt, Bailey

Ms. Frizzle's Adventures: Ancient Egypt, Cole

Mysterious Mummies, MacDonald

A Ticket to Egypt, Streissguth

Have students plan their own fantasy excursion to ancient Egypt. Map out the trip, listing connections of planes, trains, boats, or even camels. List everything they will need to bring for their trip and create an itinerary of what they will be doing once they arrive.

37. Map out Tutankhamen exhibit route

The Amazing Pop-Up Pull-Out Mummy Book, Hawcock

The Tomb of the Boy King, Frank

Gather information about the King Tut exhibit. How are his remains and other artifacts being preserved? Make a map of the exhibit route, destinations, and dates. Have students create a flyer about the exhibit including facts about King Tut's life, artifacts included in the exhibit, and the map of the exhibit route. Discuss why it is important to have an opportunity to study the exhibit and the Egyptian culture.

38. Create a character web about Hatshepsut

Hatshepsut, His Majesty, Herself, Andronik

Have students create a web of Hatshepsut's personality traits noting strengths, weaknesses, accomplishments, and difficulties she had to overcome.

39. Explore the pyramids

Mummies Made in Egypt, Aliki

You Wouldn't Want to Be an Egyptian Mummy! Disgusting Things You'd Rather Not Know, Stewart

Have students compile an inventory of everything that was placed in the pyramid with the pharaoh, after his death. Discuss the reason for each item. What did the Egyptians believe about the afterlife? Have students discuss important items they would place in a pyramid to take into the afterlife, as a person living during ancient Egyptian times. For more information also see NOVA Online/Pyramids – The Inside Story at <pbs.org/wgbh/nova/pyramid/>.

Art Arena

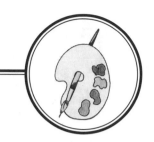

Focusing on King Tutankhamen

Tutankhamen's Gift, Sabuda

In 1922, British archaeologist Howard Carter discovered Tutankhamen's burial chamber in the Valley of the Kings. The nearly untouched tomb's contents helped us learn about King Tut, and about ancient Egyptian lifestyle and culture. Today, King Tut's traveling exhibit shares these treasures with museum goers all over the world. Egyptian art is filled with pattern, line, symmetry, and color. Robert Sabuda's *Tutankhamen's Gift* is filled with details found in traditional Egyptian art. As you study photographs and artifacts discovered in the pyramids and burial sites, it becomes

clear that the artifacts are richly designed in symmetrical repetitive pattern. Sabuda's illustrations are painted in the same color palette you will find on many Egyptian artifacts.

After experiencing authentic ancient Egyptian museum pieces, we must remember the ancient artwork does not display the mechanical precision of our modern world. These pieces are carved from wood containing natural flaws, and the Egyptians used tools that did not allow the carving to appear perfect in dimension, measurement, or balance.

In the museum display, a phoenix was shown, which is a type of mystical bird with wings that encircle the head of the bird. The head is sometimes a falcon or other bird of prey. The talons are clutching a symbol of life. Draw a large phoenix, approximately four feet by four feet. Allow the class to design the wings with colored paper and gems in colors that complement each other. Paint the talons in gold or use gold metallic wrapping paper to form the talons. Use brightly colored paper or glitter to fill in the circle being clutched in the talons. Make it symmetrical, but allow the human imperfections to be part of the design. A sample phoenix is shown below.

The Amazing Pop-Up Pull-Out Mummy Book, Hawcock; *King Tut: Tales from the Tomb*, Briscoe; *The Tomb of the Boy King*, Frank; *Tutankhamun: The Boy King*, Gaff

Mummy Bread Sticks

Purchase a roll of breadstick dough at the grocery. Give each student one small piece to roll into a round ball to form the mummies head and a larger piece to roll into a shape about four inches long, wide enough to match the size of the head. Stick both pieces together and bake, following the directions on the bread dough package. Cool. Have students wrap the bread dough in one-inch wide strips of aluminum foil, beginning at the head and working their way down until the breadstick resembles a mummy.

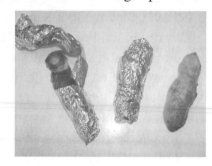

Ataif Pancakes

Look What Came from Egypt by Miles Harvey states that pancakes originated in Egypt. Below is our kid friendly adaptation for Ataif pancakes, a sweet treat served at weddings and special occasions throughout the Arabic-speaking countries.

Ingredients:

Batter
1/2 tsp. dry baking yeast
1 tsp. sugar
1-1/4 cups water
1-1/2 cups all-purpose flour

Cheese Filling
1 small carton ricotta cheese
¼ cup sugar
2 tsp. cinnamon

Directions:

Have students dissolve the yeast and sugar in water. Set aside for 5 minutes. Measure flour into a mixing bowl. Stir the yeast mixture into the flour and stir until smooth. Cover the bowl with a damp cloth and let the batter rise for 15 minutes. Lightly oil a heated griddle. Have the teacher pour a small amount of batter into the pan. Flip the pancake when small bubbles form on the surface. Have students spread a tablespoon of the ricotta cheese mixture over their own pancakes and sprinkle with sugar and cinnamon. Ataif pancakes may be served hot or cold, with syrup.

Culminating Activities

Cleopatra and the Pharaoh, a play
Life in Ancient Egypt, Challen

Act out *Cleopatra and the Pharaoh*

After learning about the social hierarchy of ancient Egyptians, have students perform the Egyptian play, *Cleopatra and the Pharaoh*. The production incorporates a student generated set and props. See figure 3.67 *Cleopatra and the Pharaoh Script* on page 122 for the play script and figure 3.66 *Prop Setting* guide on page 121.

Following the play, actors serve as museum curators, each sharing the significance of one of the many props completed in preparation for the play.

Props List

Play invitations and program - Cut and glue geometric shapes onto the front cover of the invitation and program. The inside of the invitations should include the day and time of the play. Inside the front cover of the program is a keepsake photo of children dressed in their costumes. The opposite page includes the play title, date of performance, and a list of play parts matched with children playing those parts.

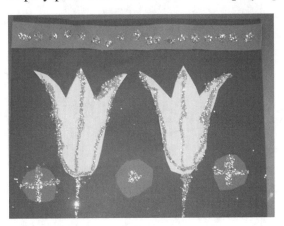

Two thrones - The pharaoh and his wife each have a throne. Thrones should be mounted on a step up from the main floor, as the pharaoh and his wife are on center stage throughout the play.

Palace walls - Students wrap several boxes of the same size in white paper and decorate with hieroglyphics. Boxes are stacked to form a wall on both sides of the thrones.

Five foot long sarcophagus - Students follow directions for *Making a Sarcophagus* that can be found in the Fine Arts section of Curriculum Connections, project #4

Four tall columns - Use four large tubes for columns. Set on side stage, with the sarcophagus in front, so it looks like a burial tent outside the palace. Cover the column with white paper and decorate with Egyptian shapes. This is a great exercise in symmetry and pattern.

Palm trees - Students cut large leaf shapes, planning six to eight per tree. Tape a stiff wire the length of the leaf, allowing the end of the wire to extend about eight inches beyond to create a stem. The wire is then bent and placed in the end of the tube. Students should paint the tube brown to look like a tree trunk. To stand the trees up easily and make them easy to relocate, stand the tree trunk on a plastic milk jug and fill with sand.

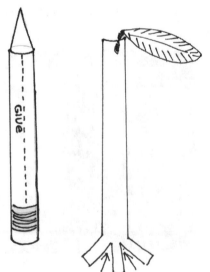

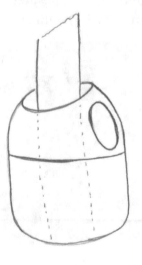

Egyptian sky backdrop - Pin a piece of dark blue paper on the wall the width of your stage. Use bright pastels in colors of a morning sky, such as shocking pink, orange, and magenta. Have students create wide colored stripes along the paper by dragging pastels. Then students rub each stripe with their hands to blend the colors. Hands get dirty, but pastels are easily washed off.

Finger chimes and ankle bells - To make ankle bells, have performers string jingle bells to tie around their ankles.

Carriage - Students decorate a wagon in which the pharaoh and Cleopatra ride.

Ribbons - Layer three multi-colored ribbons. Fold in the center. Sew ribbons together six inches from the center of the fold, to create a handle that is easy to hold on to and wave.

Collar for Cleopatra - Students create a collar by stringing sparkly beads, long enough to slip over the cat's head.

Wax for Cleopatra's head - The wax for Cleopatra's head can be made from a small paper cup held on by double stick tape.

Cleopatra's props - A ball of yarn is needed for Cleopatra to play with during the final song.

Cleopatra's rug
Egypt: The Culture, Moscovitch
Cut a circle large enough for Cleopatra to perform. Have students decorate it with rows of colorful repetitive patterns. Strengthen the completed rug by covering it with clear packing tape.

Priest's props - A candle and a jar of oil are needed to serve as a jar of holy oil.

Stone carver's tools - A small hammer, plastic chisel, cat statue, and table on which to carve are needed.

Artist's tools - The artist carries a palette of paints, paintbrush, and finished picture of a cat on stage.

Weaver's equipment - The weaver carries a basket on stage and drops a ball of yarn from the basket.

Costumes - Simple costumes can be made from large pieces of fabric. The girls' gowns are made by measuring the height of the child from floor to shoulder.

Double the measurement and that will be the length of the fabric piece. Fold the fabric from top to bottom, cutting a small circle for the neck. Measure six to eight inches from the top shoulder down. Pin and sew side seam from that spot to the hem on both sides. String a ribbon through the neck hole and out the sleeve. Tie it tightly over the shoulder, cinching up the fabric to gather it down the front and back of the dress. For the boys' costumes, measure the waist. Add

six inches and glue a hook and loop piece to fit the child. Each boy's headdress is made by cutting a piece of fabric wide enough to fit around his head, and at least 18 inches long. Place it on the child's forehead and attach the fabric together behind his head, allowing the excess to drape down the back. See pattern, figure 3.82 *Dress Headdress Pattern* in template section on page 125.

Ancient Egypt Assessment Rubric

Students will be able to:	Fair 1	Good 2	Mastered 3	Score
Locate Egypt, the Sahara Desert and the Nile River on a map				
Understand the meanings and uses of sarcophagus, canopic jars, and Book of the Dead				
Recognize how the Rosetta Stone impacted the translation of the hieroglyphic language				
Explain the Egyptian beliefs associated with the amulet				
Realize the importance of the discovery of King Tut to the modern world				
Share some facts about the pyramids, mastabas and shabtis				
Identify some foods of that time period				
Compare ancient Egyptian lifestyles to modern day				
Describe the meaning of cartouche and for whom they were used				

Figure 3.109 Egypt Rubric

Multimedia Resources

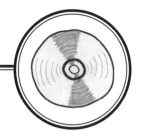

Egyptian Treasures: Mummies and Myths [sound recording].
Greathall Productions, Inc., 1999. 60 min.

> This treasury of Egyptian tales, created and told by award-winning storyteller Jim Weiss, includes *The Great Myths of Egypt, Osiris, The Secret Name of Ra-Amun, A Rival for the Throne, The Courage of Isis, The Pyramid Builders*, and *The Mummy's Tomb* (Grades 2-6).

Mummies Made in Egypt [video recording] produced by LeVar Burton. Episode 54: Reading Rainbow: GPN/ Nebraska Educational Telecommunications, 2001-2003. 30 min.

> Host LeVar Burton takes viewers to the Museum of Fine Arts in Boston to explore Egyptian mummies. A CAT scan shows what a mummy looks like after thousands of years (Grades 3-6).

Pavarotti's Opera Made Easy-My Favourite Opera for Children [sound recording]. London Philharmonic Orchestra, et al. Decca, 1994.

> The world's greatest tenor introduces children to his favorite operas including *Madame Butterfly, Hansel and Gretel,* and *Aida*. What better way to introduce children to the story of *Aida,* then to have them listen to a song from the opera composed by Giuseppe Verdi and performed by Rome Opera Orchestra and Chorus, *Aida: Triumphal Choruses and March* (Grades K-6).

Tutankhamun-Tut: The Boy King [DVD]. Monterey video: Distributed by Monterey Media, Inc., 2005. 60 min.

> This award-winning documentary on the discovery and contents of King Tut's tomb exhibit highlights Howard Carter's 1922 discovery in the Valley of the Kings, and features information about King Tutankhamun's mysterious life and death (Grades 3-8).

The Detroit Institute of Arts: Ancient Art <www.dia.org/collections/ancient/egypt/egypt. html>

Learn more about the Egyptian beliefs and afterlife by examining ancient art examples of canopic jars, mummies, holy animals, the Book of the Dead, and tombs.

Egypt: Gift of the Nile <www.seattleartmuseum.org/Exhibit/Archive/egypt/discover/default. htm>

Here you will find online activities for children to explore the world of the ancient Egyptians. Choose a wig for the Egyptian barber, explore the ancient city Memphis with eight-year-old Soha, and visit a virtual temple.

Enchanted Learning <www.enchantedlearning.com/artists/egypt.shtml>

Informational Egyptian coloring pages and an Egyptian research quiz can be found at this site.

Guardian's Ancient Egypt <http://guardians.net/egypt/index.html>

This site has a vast amount of information on hieroglyphs, mummies, pyramids, and a section about the Rosetta Stone. It also includes a children's section with interactive links.

KidsZine <www.kidszine.co.uk/Egyptians.htm>

Information and links on Egyptian mythology, math, and history are found at this site.

Mark Millmore's Ancient Egypt <www.eyelid.co.uk/index.htm>

This is a great site with lots of information on hieroglyphs, pyramids, kings, and queens. There are stories, games, and interactive maps. You can download a sample print program to create 3-D crafts and board games. There are dozens of Egypt related links for one stop surfing.

National Geographic: Secrets of Egypt <www.nationalgeographic.com/pyramids/>

Participate in an online adventure as you explore how the pyramids were built, and what's inside. You can enter the shrine of the famous boy king, Tutankhamen. There is a children's section with more activities and a teacher's section with ideas and lesson plans.

NOVA Online/Pyramids – The Inside Story <www.pbs.org/wgbh/nova/pyramid/>

Explore QuickTime VR movies of the great pyramids and the sphinx. Investigate who built the pyramids and why, as you learn about ancient Egypt.

Virtual Egypt

Make your own cartouche with the hieroglyphic translator. Build a virtual pyramid, and then check out the photo gallery.

Book Resources

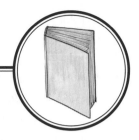

Fiction Books

The 5,000-Year-Old Puzzle: Solving a Mystery of Ancient Egypt
by Claudia Logan. Illus. Melissa Sweet. Farrar Straus Giroux, 2002.
Depicted through journal entries, postcards, and descriptive sidebars, Will Hunt and his family join Egyptologist Dr. George Reisner on an archaeological dig in Giza, where they unearth an empty sarcophagus belonging to Queen Hetep-heres (Grades K-4).

Adventures in Ancient Egypt
by Linda Bailey. Illus. Bill Slavin. Kids Can Press, 2000.
The Binkerton twins encounter the Good Times Travel Agency and begin an adventure to ancient Egypt that includes pyramids, mummies, and people from the past (Grades 2-4).

Aida
told by Leontyne Price. Illus. Leo and Diane Dillon. Harcourt, Brace, Jovanovich, Publishers, 1990.
The love of an Ethiopian princess for an Egyptian general results in tragedy in this retelling of Verdi's opera. When captured by Egyptian soldiers, Aida must choose between loyalty to her father and country, or true love (Grades 1-4).

Bill and Pete Go Down the Nile
by Tomie dePaola. G.P. Putnam's Sons, 1987.
While on a class field trip down the Nile to study the sphinx, mummies, and a sarcophagus, a crocodile and his bird serving as a toothbrush enter a pyramid and end up saving the Sacred Eye of Isis from falling into evil hands (Grades K-2).

Croco'nile
by Roy Gerrard. Farrar, Straus & Giroux, 1994.
Hamut and his sister, Nekatu, stow away on a boat and end up in a strange city where they discover their talents for sculpting and painting. The children are nearly abducted when the plans of their would be abductors are foiled by a storm, and a crocodile they befriended earlier in the story happens by to carry them home (Grades K-2).

The Egyptian Cinderella
by Shirley Climo. Illus. Ruth Heller. Thomas Y. Crowell, 1989.
When the falcon drops a rose-red slipper into the pharaoh's lap, Amasis's search for the

maiden with a lost slipper begins in this 16th century Egyptian rendition of Cinderella (Grades K-3).

The Egyptian News: The Greatest Newspaper in Civilization

by Scott Steedman. Gareth Stevens Publishing, 2000.
"Queen Rocks Nation," "Boy-King Dies," and "The Nile: A Special Report," are just a few of the newspaper articles capturing historical events and ancient Egyptian activities in this lively oversized book created in newspaper format (Grades 2-4).

Ghosts of the Nile

by Cheryl Harness. Simon & Schuster Books for Young Readers, 2004.
While on an exciting journey through ancient Egypt with his great aunt, Zachary enters a "Do Not Enter," door at a museum exhibit and, guided by a talking cat, learns about pyramid construction, great Egyptian pharaohs, and the mummification process (Grades 2-4).

Gift of the Nile: An Ancient Egyptian Legend

retold by Jan M. Mike. Illus. Charles Reasoner. Troll Associates, 1993.
While on a magical boat ride down the Nile River, Mutemwia proves her friendship to the pharaoh, who offers her freedom and a house near the palace, and proclaims the golden lotus she has rescued to be forever a sign of his pledge of love to her (Grades K-2).

I Am the Mummy Heb-Nefert

by Eve Bunting. Illus. David Christiana. Harcourt Brace & Company, 1997.
Told in first person, a mummy entombed in a glass case for viewing by museum visitors recalls the story of her life and death as Heb-Nefert, the once beautiful wife of the pharaoh's brother (Grades 2-4).

I, Crocodile

by Fred Marcellino. HarperCollins Publishers: Michael Di Capua Books, 1999.
After robbing Egypt of mummies and other landmarks, Napoleon ships them to Paris, along with a crocodile to display. The crocodile enjoys entertaining crowds, but his appetite for larger portions of French cuisine leads him to slip through the sewers of Paris, where he now dines on whomever he wants. Magnificent illustrations capture the aristocratic settings (Grades K-3).

Ms. Frizzle's Adventures: Ancient Egypt

by Joanna Cole. Illus. Bruce Degen. Scholastic Press, 2001.
Separated from their guide, Ms. Frizzle and her tour group end up in ancient Egypt, where they build a pyramid and witness the making of a mummy (Grades K-3).

Mummy Riddles

by Katy Hall and Lisa Eisenberg. Illus. Nicole Rubel. The Penguin Group: Puffin Books, 1997.

Included are a selection of humorous riddles such as, "What did the mummy say when he got angry with a skeleton?" and "I have a bone to pick with you" (Grades K-3).

Mysterious Mummies

by Fiona MacDonald. Gareth Stevens Publishing, 2004.

Written in journal format, readers are invited to accompany fictitious characters, Will Yates and Dr. Jane Smith, on a journey where they learn factual information about the work of Egyptologists, archaeologists, and scientists (Grades 2-4).

Nefertari: Princess of Egypt

by Roberta Angeletti. Oxford University Press, 1998.

While on tour at Egypt's Valley of the Queens, young Anna follows a cat into the tomb of Egyptian princess, Nefertari, who comes to life and gives her a brief education in Egyptian culture (Grades K-3).

The Star-Bearer: A Creation Myth from Ancient Egypt

by Dianne Hofmeyr. Illus. Jude Daly. Farrar Straus Giroux, 2001.

When the godchild Atum is hindered in his creation by an inseparable god and goddess, he is forced to separate the god of earth from the god of sky, leaving one furious and the other lonely. Thoth, the god of all wisdom, finds a way to help Nut have children in the five light days granted to her, and Osiris, Horus, Set, Isis, and Nephthys are born (Grades 2-4).

Who Built the Pyramid?

by Meredith Hooper. Illus. Robin Heighway-Bury. Candlewick, 2001.

Who built the pyramid? The quarry master, foreman, laborers, water carrier, stone mason, and sculptor each weigh in with claims of their roles in building Senwosret's pyramid (Grades 2-4).

Zekmet, the Stone Carver: A Tale of Ancient Egypt

by Mary Stolz. Illus. Deborah Nourse Lattimore. Harcourt Brace Jovanovich, 1988.

Stolz weaves a story about an unknown stone carver, who is asked to build a monument to honor a vein pharaoh. Part man, part lion, the Sphinx symbolizes Egyptian power, the pharaoh's pride, and the unknown stone carver's skill (Grades 1-3).

Zoom Upstream

by Tim Wynne-Jones. Illus. Eric Beddows. HarperCollins Publishers, 1992.
When Zoom the cat follows Maria's footsteps to the library, he ends up going through a bookshelf that leads him down a trail of books to the Nile River in ancient Egypt, where he joins his friend Maria in search of his Uncle Roy (Grades K-2).

Information Books

100 Things You Should Know About Ancient Egypt

by Jane Walker. Mason Crest Publishers, 2003.
Royal news, powerful people, magnificent monuments, mummies, and games are all dealt with in bite-size pieces, enhanced with lively illustrations (Grades K-4).

1001 Facts About Ancient Egypt

by Scott Steedman. DK Publishing, Inc., 2003.
Included in this handbook are fascinating facts about ancient Egyptian society, daily life, games, building and technology, religion, and the end of an era (Grades 2-6).

The Amazing Pop-Up Pull-Out Mummy Book

by David Hawcock. Illus. Claire Bampton. Paper engineered and designed by David Hawcock. Dorling Kindersley Publishing, Inc., 2000.
A five-foot-high pop-up of King Tutankhamen brings facts about mummies around the world to life through its life-size portrayal and vivid illustrations (Grades 2-4).

Ancient Egypt

by Neil D. Bramwell. Enslow Publishers, Inc. A MyReportLinks.com Book, 2004.
Report links, a time line, and coverage of land, people, and cultural contributions are some of the highlights of this book designed for young researchers (Grades 3-5).

Ancient Egypt

by John Malam. Enchanted Lion Books, 2004.
Ancient Egyptian sites, objects, landscape, government, work, beliefs, families, homes, and culture are covered in this informative book that includes a timeline (Grades 2-6).

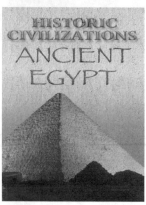

The Atlas of Ancient Egypt

by Neil Morris. Illus. Paola Ravaglia et al. Peter Bedrick Books, 2000.

Readers are offered a glimpse of pyramid builders, gods and goddesses, death and afterlife, and daily life and culture of Ancient Egypt (Grades 2-6).

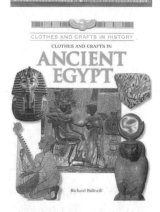

Builders and Craftsmen

by Jane Shuter. Heinemann Library, 1999.

The lives and work of the builders and craftsmen who built the pyramids are studied, focusing on how they did it, the tools they used, and how they were compensated for their work (Grades 2-4).

Cat Mummies

by Kelly Trumble. Illus. Laszlo Kubinyi. Clarion Books, 1996.

This heavily researched text explains the process of mummification as well as why cats were worshipped in ancient Egypt, displayed as totems, and mummified (Grades 2-4).

Clothes and Crafts in Ancient Egypt

by Richard Balkwill. Gareth Stevens Publishing, 2000.

This introduction to ancient Egyptian crafts, clothing, jewelry, and festivals includes games, a glossary, and a section of recommended books (Grades 1-4).

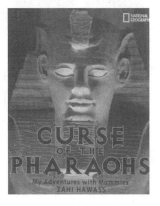

Curse of the Pharaohs: My Adventures with Mummies

by Zahi Hawass. National Geographic, 2004.

The director of Excavations at Giza Pyramids captivates older readers with true stories of Ancient Egypt's treasures, mysteries, and archaeology (Grades 4-Adult).

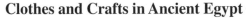

Egypt

by David and Patricia Armentrout. Rourke Publishing LLC, 2004.

Egyptian myths, society, and powerful women are just a few of the topics covered, spanning 3100-30 BC to the end of an empire 332-30 BCE (Grades 1-3).

Egypt

by Christy Steele. Raintree Steck-Vaughn Publishers: Steadwell Books, 2001.

This introduction to Egyptian culture includes history, government, food, and farming, as well as a selection of Internet sites and useful addresses to encourage student learning (Grades K-3).

Egypt In Spectacular Cross-Section

by Stewart Ross. Illus. Stephen Biesty. Scholastic: Scholastic Non-fiction, 2005.

Eleven-year-old Dedia and his father are transported back to ancient Egypt where they travel the Nile River during a 30-day expedition in 1230 BCE (Grades K-4).

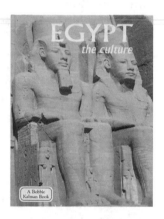

Egypt: The Culture

by Arlene Moscovitch. Crabtree Publishing Company, 2000.

Egyptian life, pyramids, mummies, King Tut, hieroglyphs, beliefs, religion, music, dance, art, and stories of gods and Pharaohs are part of the fare (Grades 2-4).

Egyptian Mummies

by Henrietta McCall. Illus. David Antram. Franklin Watts, 2000.

Every aspect of Egyptian mummies is explored from death and burial to preparation, coffins, the funeral procession, stocking the tomb with treasures, and tomb robbers (Grades 2-4).

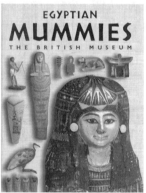

Egyptian Mummies: People from the Past

by Delia Pemberton. Photographs by the British Museum Photographic Service et al. Harcourt, Inc., 2001.

Life and death in ancient Egypt unfold as we examine the remains of seven mummies from the British Museum. What they looked like, the foods they ate, and why they prepared for the afterlife, as they did, are depicted (Grades 2-8).

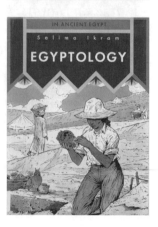

Egyptology

by Salima Ikram. Illus. Riham El Sherbini. Hoopoe Books, 1997.

The work of Egyptologists, how they recreate the past, and a

study of the language, history, art, and culture of the ancient Egyptians is the focus of *Egyptology* (Grades 2-6).

Egyptology: Search for the Tomb of Osiris

edited by Emily Sands and Dugald A. Steer. Illus. Nick Harris and Helen Ward. Candlewick Press, 2004.

This journal of Ms. Emily Sands is an undocumented facsimile of a journal supposedly written in 1926, filled with envelopes, pockets, hieroglyphs, postcards, and small treasures, assembled in scrapbook format (Grades 2-6).

Gods and Goddesses in the Daily Life of the Ancient Egyptians

by Henrietta McCall. Illus. John James. McGraw-Hill Children's Publishing: Peter Bedrick Books, 2002.

This book discusses how belief in gods and goddesses of ancient Egypt helped mold the lives and culture of the Egyptian people (Grades 2-6).

Going to War in Ancient Egypt

by Dr. Anne Millard. Franklin Watts: Grolier Publishing, 2000.

Ancient Egyptian armies, fortresses, weapons, and armor are addressed (Grades 2-4).

Hatshepsut, His Majesty, Herself

by Catherine M. Andronik. Illus. Joseph Daniel Fiedler. Atheneum Books for Young Readers, 2001.

This picture book biography details the life of Egypt's only successful female pharaoh, Hatshepsut, who reigned for over 20 years (Grades 2-4).

King Tut: Tales from the Tomb

by Diana C. Briscoe. Capstone Curriculum Publishing, 2003.

Focusing on life after death, this book discusses ancient Egyptian customs, beliefs, and legends, the process of mummification, and King Tut (Grades 2-6).

Life in Ancient Egypt

by Paul Challen. Crabtree Publishing Company, 2005.

Ancient Egyptian life is explored through language, values, life after death, art and pastimes, scientific innovations and pyramids (Grades 2-4).

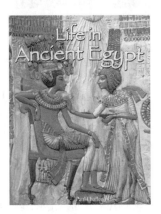

Look What Came from Egypt

by Miles Harvey. Grolier Publishing: Franklin Watts, 1998.

Egyptian inventions, fashion, food, toys and games, animals, musical instruments, and recipes are the focus of this inviting book about Egyptian innovations (Grades 1-4).

Mummies and Ancient Egypt

by Anita Ganeri. Gareth Stevens Publishing, 2005.
Contents include information about the Nile River, mummies, gods and temples, the pharaoh, pyramids, Egyptian life, fashion, school days, and work (Grades K-4).

Mummies Made in Egypt

by Aliki. Harper & Row Publishers: A Harper Trophy Book, 1979.
Aliki uses line drawings and minimal text to detail the process of mummification and explain why Egyptians buried their dead in this manner (Grades 2-5).

Mummies, Pyramids, and Pharaohs: A Book About Ancient Egypt

by Gail Gibbons. Little, Brown and Company, 2003.
Through line drawings, maps, and minimal text, Gibbons shares a wealth of information about ancient Egypt, spanning pharaohs to hieroglyphics (Grades K-2).

Mummies Unwrapped!

by Kimberly Weinberger. Illus. Portia Sloan. Scholastic Inc., 2001.
This high interest reader discusses life and death in ancient Egypt (Grades 1-3).

Pyramids

by Teresa Hyman. Thomson Gale: Kidhaven Press, 2005.
Readers learn about the location, purpose, and contents of famous pyramids (Grades 2-6).

Pyramids & Mummies

by Seymour Simon. SeaStar Books, 2003.
This book offers an overview of Egyptian pyramid construction and discusses Ancient Egyptian burial practices (Grades 2-4).

A Ticket to Egypt

by Thomas Streissguth. Carolrhoda Books, 1999.
Current day Egyptian culture including homes, religion, sports, and music are the focus of this inviting book (Grades 1-3).

Writing in Ancient Egypt

by Jil Fine. The Rosen Publishing Group, Inc., 2003.
Hieroglyphics, hieratic writing, demotic writing, and the Rosetta Stone are discussed in a format that is simple for younger students to understand (Grades 1-3).

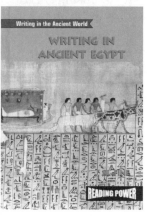

You Wouldn't Want to Be an Egyptian Mummy! Disgusting Things You'd Rather Not Know

by David Stewart. Illus. David Antram. Grolier Publishing: Franklin Watts, 2000/2003.
This book takes a look at the art of ancient Egyptian burial including mummification, tombs and tomb robbers, animal mummies, and the afterlife (Grades 3-6).

Biography Books • King Tutankhamen (Art Arena Focus)

The Tomb of the Boy King

by John Frank. Illus. Tom Pohrt. Farrar Straus Giroux: Frances Foster Books, 2001.
Information about the boy king is revealed as this story details Howard Carter and Lord Carnarvon's efforts to find King Tutankhamen's tomb and discoveries in the Valley of the Kings (Grades 2-6).

Tutankhamen's Gift

by Robert Sabuda. Atheneum, 1994.
Sabuda combines simple text with exquisite artwork to tell the story of a frail member of the royal family who would become pharaoh at the age of ten, restore the temples, and rule over his people with a kind heart (Grades K-2).

Tutankhamun: The Boy King

by Jackie Gaff. Illus. Anthony Lewis. Peter Bedrick Books, 2003.
The story of King Tutankhamun's life unfolds with final pages discussing discovery of the young prince's long lost tomb and treasures (Grades K-3).

Activity Books

The Egyptians

by Rachel Wright. Sea-to-Sea Publications, 2005.
Historical facts and relevant activities including a water clock, scarab stamp seal, fish charm, Egyptian wig, and coffins are part of this colorful hands-on book, designed to help children learn more about ancient Egypt (Grades 2-4).

Pyramids! 50 Hands-On Activities to Experience Ancient Egypt

by Avery Hart and Paul Mantell. Illus. Michael Kline. Williamson Publishing, 1997.
Activities designed to help students experience ancient Egypt include hieroglyphics, the Riddle of the Sphinx, clay pyramids, and an Egyptian costume party (Grades 2-6).

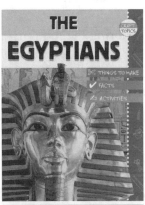

Pyramids: A Fascinating Learn-It-Yourself Project Book

by Peter Mellett. Gareth Stevens Publishing, 1999.
Math and Science projects are utilized to determine the properties and strength of pyramid shapes and the construction of pyramids (Grades 2-6).

The Mummy's Curse

by Steve Presser

"Beware of the mummy's curse.
If you don't then you shall die!"
Covering my mouth, I looked at the man
And jokingly said, "Oh my!"

"Beware of the mummy's curse,
For death may come to haunt you."
Chuckling a little, I raised my hands
And said to the man, "Oooooooh!"

Ignoring the mummy's curse,
I opened the tomb up wide.
Then tickling King Tut, I pulled his bandage,
And played with the jewelry inside.

"Beware of the mummy's curse!"
Screamed the man as he ran and hid.
"But the curse isn't real!" I yelled to the man.
"Who cares if I opened the lid?"

Figure 3.45 The Mummy's Curse

Prop Setting

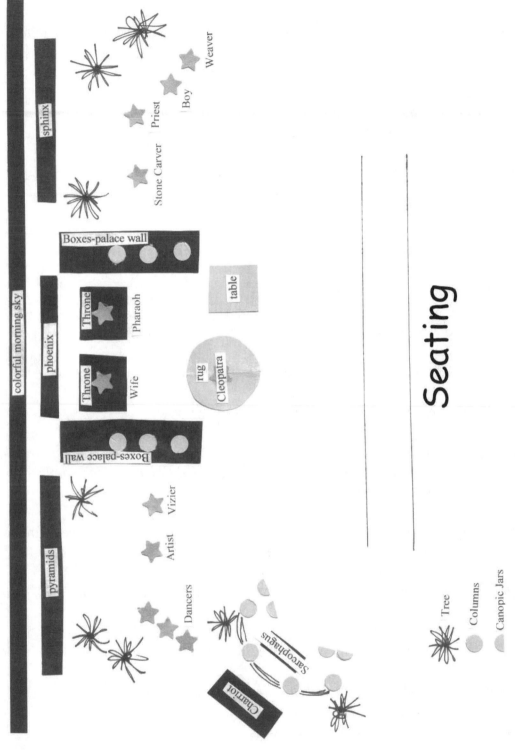

Figure 3.66 Prop Setting

Cleopatra and the Pharaoh Play Script

Teacher: Welcome to our play. It is called Cleopatra because we have been learning about ancient Egypt and Cleopatra was the name of an Egyptian Queen.

Narrator: After rising, early in the morning the Pharaoh went into the throne room to sit and relax. He liked playing with his cat every morning but this day something was terribly wrong.

Narrator exits center stage as the Pharaoh stretches, yawns, and enters the throne room and sits on his throne. The wife follows the pharaoh onto center stage and sits on her throne also.

Pharaoh: Oh what a beautiful day it is Cleopatra. Here, come sit with me.

Kitty: Meow, meow, meow.

Cleopatra looks very disinterested and stays on her beautiful rug.

Pharaoh: Cleopatra! Aren't you feeling well?

Cleopatra: Meooow (Very sad)

Pharaoh: Wife, Cleo isn't well! Please help her. Do something to make her better.

Wife: I will dress her in jewels and put fragrant wax on her head.

The wife approaches Cleopatra with a necklace and quickly puts it around Cleopatra's neck. Then wife places the wax on Cleopatra's head making sure the hook and loop attaches before leaving. Wife looks at Cleopatra and pets her gently.

Wife: Cleo still isn't well. I'll find the vizier to heal her. Vizier, vizier, come to the throne room to heal Cleopatra because she isn't feeling well.

The vizier enters the throne room, looks at Cleopatra, and says in a stuffy voice with an air of unconcern.

Vizier: I will help you, Cleopatra, as soon as the Pharaoh tells me what he wants me to do.

The vizier looks at the pharaoh and waits for directions from him.

Pharaoh: Me! I want you to have your own ideas to heal Cleopatra!

The Pharaoh sounds very indignant.

Figure 3.67 Cleopatra and the Pharaoh Play Script

Vizier: In that case, I'll get the priest. Priest! Priest! Come to the palace to heal Cleopatra.

Priest enters very solemn. He glances at the cat and begins to pray.

Priest: I pray to the gods of all heaven and earth and I pray to all the gods of the underworld. Come to heal Cleopatra for my Pharaoh.

The priest looks at Cleo and is surprised that she isn't any better.
Kitty is beginning to appear even sadder and lays her head down on her rug.

Priest: My dear Pharaoh! Cleopatra still isn't well. I'll find someone to help! Hurry! Send in the dancers to make her feel better.

The dancers come in and sit around Cleopatra.

Dancer 1: Cleopatra we will dance for you and you will feel better soon.

Dancers all get up and dance around in front of Cleopatra ringing finger cymbals and ankle bells. When the dance is done they sit around Cleopatra looking concerned.

Dancer 2: How are you feeling now, Cleopatra?

Dancer 3: Pharaoh, we have danced for Cleo but she doesn't seem to care.

All dancers: We will find someone to help! Stone carver! Stone carver!

Dancer 2: Can you carve a statue for Cleopatra that will make her feel better?

Stone carver enters as the dancers dance off stage. He brings with him a tray with a block of plaster that hides a small statue of a cat. Stone carver looks at Cleopatra, walks around her, measures her, and then sets to his carving work. He taps his hammer on the chisel to make the sound of chiseling as he whistles or hums a short song. Finally, he puts down his tools and lifts up his finished carving. He shows Cleopatra his carving and Cleopatra meows and claws toward the carving. Cleopatra lies her head down wearily, and acts very sad and sick.

Stone carver: Pharaoh, my beautiful carving hasn't healed Cleo. I was sure it would make her purr. I will call for the artist to paint a picture for her. Artist! Artist! Come to the palace to paint a portrait for Cleopatra.

Artist enters and cuddles with Cleopatra.

Artist: Dear little Cleopatra. I have been told you are very ill. I will paint a portrait for you. I'm sure it will make you happy.

The artist goes quickly to the side of the stage and quickly paints a portrait of a cat. She returns to show Cleopatra the painting. Cleopatra responds by meowing long and mournfully.

Artist: Cleopatra you look even sicker than before. I will call the weaver to make a gown for you to wear into the afterlife.

Weaver enters and measures Cleopatra for her gown; then she sits and begins to weave the gown.

Weaver: Come Cleo, I will make a fabulous gown for you to wear. All the gods will envy your beautiful gown.

As the weaver begins her work she drops a small ball of yarn in front of Cleopatra. She notices the yarn and lifts her head to look at it. The boy (the weaver's son) picks up the yarn and dangles it in front of Cleopatra. Cleopatra jumps off her rug and chases the yarn as the boy runs back and forth. Cleopatra meows over and over as the boy laughs and jumps.

Boy: Come on Cleo, jump and chase. Ha, ha, jump and chase. Ha, ha jump and chase. Why Cleopatra, you aren't sick at all! You just want to play.

Pharaoh: You have healed Cleopatra for me! I have never seen her so happy and well! I think all she needed was a boy to play with. Please come to the palace everyday to play with Cleo and I will pay you handsomely. Let's celebrate, for Cleopatra has been healed!

The pharaoh and Cleopatra board the special chariot. The vizier pulls the wagon or chariot around the stage, while all the town's people celebrate with music and cries of happiness. The celebration should be loud and exciting and a grand finale for the play.

The class lines up to take a bow and sing a song.

Dress and Headdress Patterns

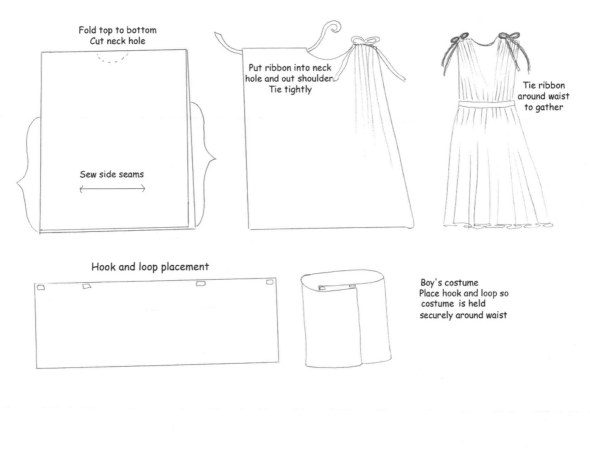

Fold top to bottom
Cut neck hole

Sew side seams

Put ribbon into neck hole and out shoulder. Tie tightly

Tie ribbon around waist to gather

Hook and loop placement

Boy's costume
Place hook and loop so costume is held securely around waist

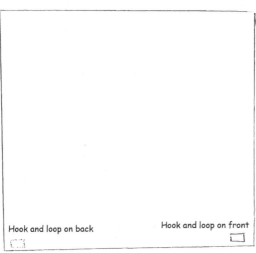

Hook and loop on back

Hook and loop on front

Wrap headdress around head and hook together in the back. Drape fabric down the back behind ears.

Figure 3.82 Dress and Headdress Patterns

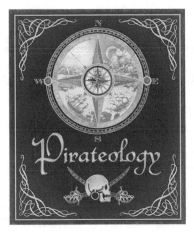

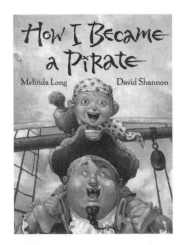

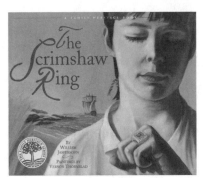

Travel Itinerary

Classroom Setting

Classroom Setting Supplies	Word Wall	
telescope	ratline	mutiny
pirate hats	crow's nest	figurehead
Jolly Roger	maroon	logbook
ship's wheel	cutlass	landlubber
heavy rope	booty	scurvy
barrel	Jolly Roger	mast
treasure chest	hardtack	
chain		
pirate books		
cardboard pirate ship		
cardboard tube swords		
flour bags filled with fiberfill for pillows		

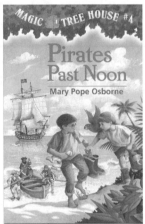

Magic Tree House Book Annotations

Pirates Past Noon

by Mary Pope Osborne. Illus. Sal Murdocca. Random House, 1994.
When Jack and Annie return to the tree house they discover a book open to a picture of a sunny beach, parrot in a palm tree, and a ship sailing on the sea. Wishing they were there on such a rainy day, the tree house whisks them off to a new adventure in the midst of pirate time. After dealing with pirates and in search of a treasure, the two return home to Frog Creek, where Morgan le Fay reveals herself to them (Grades K-3).

Pirates

by Will Osborne and Mary Pope Osborne. Illus. Sal Murdocca. Random House, 2001.
This nonfiction companion to *Pirates Past Noon* is filled with interesting facts about pirates including information about pirates in history, pirate ships, pirate treasure, and authentic pirate stories (Grades K-3).

Connecting with Magic Tree House Books

Pirates Past Noon Critical Thinking Questions

1. Which clues helped Jack and Annie figure out where the tree house landed?
2. What led Cap'n Bones to believe Jack and Annie knew where the treasure was buried?
3. How did Annie figure out where the treasure was hidden?
4. What kept Jack on the island longer than he should have stayed?
5. What happened to Polly the Parrot when the tree house landed back in Frog Creek, Pennsylvania?

Pirates Past Noon Curriculum Connections

1. Journal three clues about the "M" person

Jack and Annie collected three clues about the "M" person. After reading about their list of clues, have students check their own Magic Tree House journals to make sure that they have listed all three.

2. Search the Internet for facts

Create a fact sheet about the author of the Magic Tree House series, Mary Pope Osborne, and author of the research guides, Will Osborne. Investigate how Mary Pope Osborne became involved in writing the Magic Tree House series?

3. Locate Frog Creek, Pennsylvania

Jack and Annie live in Frog Creek, Pennsylvania. Have students look on a map of Pennsylvania to see if it is a real or imaginary place.

4. Investigate having a pet parrot

After looking at one of the books inside the tree house, Jack and Annie see a parrot outside the window sitting on a branch. Use the Internet to investigate the care it takes to own a parrot and calculate the costs involved. Cost should include the parrot and items such as a cage and food. Decide if a parrot would be a suitable pet for the classroom or library.

5. Imagine being on the beach

In the story, Jack and Annie visit a beach. Have students close their eyes and imagine they are on the beach with Jack and Annie. Ask them to describe what they would see, hear, taste, touch, and smell. As a follow-up, have students write a story detailing how they would spend the day on that beach.

6. Map out islands in the Caribbean

The book found in the tree house that took Jack and Annie to the beach was *Pirates of the Caribbean*. Locate the Caribbean Islands. Select one of the islands and determine its latitude and longitude. As an extension, have students draw a map of the Caribbean islands.

7. Learn about Morgan le Fay

Have students journal what they have learned about Morgan le Fay. They should include information about King Arthur and Camelot.

8. Investigate Jolly Roger symbolism

Jack and Annie notice a pirate ship sailing towards the beach with a Jolly Roger flying above it. Have students draw a picture of the traditional Jolly Roger with the skull and crossbones. Investigate why pirates used those symbols to be identified as a pirate ship. The *Pirates* research guide shows additional symbols used on a Jolly Roger that could help in identifying a ship. Have students list other commonly used symbols, and tell what each symbol stands for.

Pirates Curriculum Connections

1. Look at pirate weapons

Brainstorm weapons that pirates found useful in their endeavors. Have students describe how each was used and which weapon they would choose if they were pirates living in those times. Have students find additional information in the *Pirates* research guide. As an extension, students may make pirate swords out of wrapping paper rolls, paper, jewels, and paint.

Pirate Fiction Books

The Angel and the Soldier Boy, *Collington*
Captain Abdul's Pirate School, *McNaughton*
Do Pirates Take Baths? *Tucker*
Edward and the Pirates, *McPhail* ... 15, 28
The Erie Canal Pirates, *Kimmel* ... 5, 47
Everything I Know About Pirates: A Collection
    of Made-Up Facts, Educated Guesses,
    and Silly Pictures About Bad Guys of
    the High Seas, *Lichtenheld* ... 41
Henry and the Buccaneer Bunnies, *Crimi*
How I Became a Pirate, *Long* ... 24
I Spy Treasure Hunt: A Book of
    Picture Riddles, *Marzollo* ... 4
Imagine You're a Pirate, *Clibbon* ... 1, 20
It Was a Dark and Stormy Night, *Ahlberg* ... 11
Maggie and the Pirate, *Keats* ... 7
Molly Limbo, *Hodges*
The Old Pirate of Central Park, *Priest* ... 51
On the Go with Pirate Pete and
    Pirate Joe, *Cannon* ... 22
Peggony-Po: A Whale of a Tale, *Pinkney* ... 1, 28
The Pigrates Clean Up, *Kroll* ... 2
Pirate Diary: The Journal of Jake Carpenter, *Platt* 43
Pirate Pete, *Kennedy* ... 48
Pirate Pete Sets Sail, *Jaggi* ... 3, 20, 31
Pirate Pink and Treasures of the Reef, *Day* ... 34
Pirate Treasure, *Krupinski*
Pirateology: The Pirate Hunter's Companion, *Steer*
Robin Hook, Pirate Hunter, *Kimmel* ... 19
Roger the Jolly Pirate, *Helquist* ... 30
The Scrimshaw Ring, *Jaspersohn* ... 8, 39
The Sea Chest, *Buzzeo* ... 44
Shiver Me Letters: A Pirate ABC, *Sobol* ... 9
Sindbad: From the Tales of the Thousand and One
    Nights, *Ludmila Zeman* ... 17
To Capture the Wind, *MacGill-Callahan*
Tough Boris, *Fox* ... 21

Pirate Book Web

Pirate Information Books

100 Things You Should Know
    About Pirates, *Langley* ... 7, 49
The Best Book of Pirates, *Howard* ... 45, 46
Blackbeard: Eighteenth-Century Pirate
    of the Spanish Main and
    Carolina Coast, *Weintraub*
How to Be a Pirate, *Malam* ... 7
Mystery History of a Pirate Galleon, *Finney* ... 25, 26
Pirate, *Lock* ... 13, 32, 42
Pirate, *Platt* ... 27
The Pirate Queen, *McCully*
A Pirate's Life for Me: A Day Aboard a
    Pirate's Ship *Thompson, Macintosh* ... 27, 35, 38
Pirates, *Nickles* ... 4, 6, 33
Pirates, *Steele* ... 6, 38, 42, 43, 50
Pirates! Raiders of the High Seas, *Maynard* ... 7
Pirates: Robbers of the High Seas, *Gibbons* ... 48
Sea Clocks: The Story of Longitude, *Borden* ... 35
See-Through Pirates, *Davis* ... 23, 36
Sunken Treasure, *Gibbons* ... 29
True-Life Treasure Hunts, *Donnelly* ... 29
The World of the Pirate, *Garwood* 13, 18, 27, 38, 40
You Wouldn't Want to Be a
    Pirate's Prisoner: Horrible Things
    You'd Rather Not Know, *Malam* ... 16, 33

Pirate Activity Books

The Great Pirate Activity Book, *Robins*
The Pirate's Handbook: How to Become
    a Rogue of the High Seas, *Lincoln* ... 37
Pirates, *Legendre*
Pirates, *Wright*

Pirate Anthology Books

The Barefoot Book of Pirates, *Walker* ... 10, 12
The Book of Pirates, *Hague* ... 7
The Pirate Princess and
    Other Fairy Tales, *Philip* ... 10, 12
Pirates, Ships and Sailors, *Jackson* ... 7

Fine Arts/Arts and Crafts

1. Transform your image into a pirate poster
2. Conduct a Reader's Theater
3. Build a junk sculpture
4. Locate hidden objects
5. Sing traditional pirate songs
6. Create a pirate portrait
7. Dramatize a pirate's life
8. Research scrimshaw art

Language Arts

9. Write and illustrate a pirate alphabet big book
10. Evaluate pirate fairy tales
11. Tell a story in round robin fashion
12. Compare pirate folktales from different countries
13. Investigate software piracy
14. Perform a poetry break
15. Weave an adventure
16. Design a pirate game
17. Continue the adventure of Sindbad the Sailor
18. Make pirate trading cards
19. Compare story elements
20. List supplies needed for a pirate adventure
21. Learn to deal with the death of a pet
22. Showcase collections
23. Create a Pirate Points fact book
24. Write about your own treasure

Math

25. Write your own story problem
26. Graph a treasure map
27. Navigate the high seas

Science

28. Investigate bubbles
29. Describe historical treasure finds and retrievals
30. Recognize and define ship parts
31. Understand the concept of floating and sinking
32. Investigate how history has changed navigation
33. Investigate diseases pirates encountered
34. Research and draw marine life

Pirate Curriculum Web

Social Studies

35. Determine latitude and longitude
36. Explore the world of pirates
37. Create a pirate's handbook or slideshow presentation
38. Draw up a mock pirate resume
39. Document a family heirloom
40. Analyze ship rules of conduct
41. Make a wanted poster
42. List the seven seas
43. Create a notorious pirates' timeline
44. Discuss values
45. Research the life of a woman pirate
46. Draw a map depicting the *Pirate Round* voyage
47. Trace the Erie Canal route
48. Draw a map of an imaginary island
49. Design your own pirate trivia game
50. Tie a knot
51. Call a playground truce

2. Define "lubbers" and examine pirate terminology

Cap'n Bones called Jack and Annie lubbers! What is a "lubber" and why did Cap'n Bones say that to Jack and Annie? Examine other phrases and words that were commonly used by pirates.

3. Differentiate between pirates, buccaneers, and privateers

Have students determine the differences between pirates, buccaneers, and privateers. How did each fund a long voyage, and what pirate job did each entail?

4. Investigate famous pirates

List notorious pirates found in the research guide. Have each child select one on which to report including what made them famous, a chart of their route, and ports they stopped at for supplies.

5. Become a treasure hunter

Have students investigate modern day treasure hunters. Use a chart to site shipwrecks that these treasure hunters have located. Discuss what kind of treasure they might discover and what special equipment they would need to use to raise the treasure from the bottom of the ocean. Ask students how their own lives would change if they found a real sunken pirate treasure ship.

6. Investigate continents and oceans on a globe

As a group, look at a globe to become familiar with the seven continents, oceans, and seas. Find the western and eastern hemispheres and locate the equator. Look for the northern and southern hemispheres and find lines of latitude and longitude. Discuss how pirates plotted their course and how they kept their ships on the right course.

7. Study Sir Francis Drake

After reading the story of Sir Francis Drake, explain why England considered him to be a hero, while Spain thought he was an evil pirate. Ask the class which one they think he was and why?

Station Rotations Set up stations throughout the unit to accommodate differentiated learning.

Station 1: *Science* - Investigate bubbles. Dip a variety of bubble wands in the bubble solution to see what shapes they form. #28

Station 2: *Social Studies* - Practice tying knots that were used by pirates. Use a variety of ropes to tie a bowline, the sheet bend, and the reef knot. #50

Station 3: *Language Arts* - After reading, "Walk the Plank," by Steve Presser (see page 162), practice dramatizing it as a poetry break. #14

Station 4: *Arts /Technology* - Transform your face into a pirate poster using a digital photo imported into a computer drawing program. #1

Curriculum Connections

Fine Arts/Arts and Crafts

1. Transform your image into a pirate poster
Imagine You're a Pirate, Clibbon
Peggony-Po: A Whale of a Tale, Pinkney
After viewing the sample wanted poster in *Imagine You're a Pirate*, have students use a digital photo and a computer drawing program to transform their own image into a pirate. Students should add a pirate name and print out their posters to display.

Captain Bo Sparrow

2. Conduct a Reader's Theater
The Pigrates Clean Up, Kroll
Have a small group of students serve as narrators reading verses in rhyme. The rest of the group may be the pigrates, taking turns to act out each verse as it is read.

3. Build a junk sculpture
Pirate Pete Sets Sail, Jaggi
Use the illustrations in *Pirate Pete Sets Sail* to inspire students to build their own seaworthy town from junk found around the house.

4. Locate hidden objects

I Spy Treasure Hunt: A Book of Picture Riddles, Marzollo
Pirates, Nickles

Gather a collection of I Spy books and magnifying glasses. Set up a station where students may search for hidden objects. Children may enjoy listening to *Captain Bogg & Salty: Pegleg Tango*, as they search through the books. See multimedia section for this sound recording.

5. Sing traditional pirate songs

The Erie Canal Pirates, Kimmel

After learning about the Erie Canal, sing the folk song that inspired the book. Ask students to look at other folk songs about the Erie Canal they find at <www.eriecanal.org/music.html>. How do the lyrics compare?

6. Create a pirate portrait

Pirates, Nickles
Pirates, Steele

Using a variety of art supplies such as yarn, tempera paints, pastels, or pencils, have students create their own pirate portrait. Add strips of ornately decorated paper for a picture frame.

7. Dramatize a pirate's life

100 Things You Should Know About Pirates, Langley
The Book of Pirates, Hague
How to Be a Pirate, Malam
Maggie and the Pirate, Keats
Pirates! Raiders of the High Seas, Maynard
Pirates, Ships, and Sailors, Jackson

Discuss how the new kid in *Maggie and the Pirate* used his imagination to pretend he was a pirate. What did Maggie do that indicated she was a strong girl role model? Read some of the stories from the pirate anthologies and set up a station where students may dress up and dramatize being a pirate. Include a camera, so they can take pictures of one another.

8. Research scrimshaw art

The Scrimshaw Ring, Jaspersohn

Research scrimshaw art. Where did it originate? Share some of the designs found in scrimshaw.

Language Arts

9. Write and illustrate a pirate alphabet big book

Shiver Me Letters: A Pirate ABC, Sobel

Brainstorm pirate words for the letters of the alphabet. Have each student illustrate one of the letters of the alphabet with crayons or markers on paper, or use a computer-drawing program. Compile alphabetically in a book or as a computer slideshow, and write a statement about the illustration. Example: (P is for parrot) The parrot warned the crew, "Awk! Jolly Roger on the horizon!"

10. Evaluate pirate fairy tales

The Barefoot Book of Pirates, Walker

The Pirate Princess: And Other Fairy Tales, Philip

As you read the selection of pirate fairy tales, use the chart to evaluate each tale for the seven elements of a fairy tale. Evaluate several fairy tales and graph results on a spreadsheet. Librarian or teacher use figure 4.32 *Fairy Tale Elements Chart* (see page 160).

11. Tell a story in round robin fashion

It Was a Dark and Stormy Night, Ahlberg

Turn off all the lights and tell your own *It Was a Dark and Stormy Night* story in round robin fashion, passing a flashlight to the person who is speaking. The flashlight creates an eerie atmosphere. The person who is holding it is the only one who may speak.

12. Compare pirate folktales from different countries

The Barefoot Book of Pirates, Walker

The Pirate Princess: And Other Fairy Tales, Philip

Compare "The Pirate Princess" folktale with pirate folktales from different countries, using a comparison chart that includes the story title, pirate characters, plot, and setting.

13. Investigate software piracy

Pirates, Lock

The World of the Pirate, Garwood

Software piracy is a modern type of piracy. Discuss why this is piracy and ways in which it can be stopped. As a group, brainstorm and list the harmful affects of software piracy. Examine your school or library's technology code of conduct. If you do not have one, write one. To learn more have students complete the worksheet, figure 4.33 *Software Piracy Worksheet* (see page 161). For answers visit <www.uspto.gov/go/kids/kidantipiracy.htm>

14. Perform a poetry break

After reading the poem, "Walk the Plank," by Steve Presser, have students pair up, dress in character, and perform the poem as a poetry break. Have one student dress as captain, and the other as the pirate walking the plank. Use the poem "Walk the Plank" figure 4.34 on page 162.

15. Weave an adventure

Edward and the Pirates, McPhail

Have students write an adventure in which they awaken to pirates who have taken their pirate library book. Students may draw in familiar characters from other stories, such as Peter Pan, as they weave their adventure. As an extension, have students act out their story in an impromptu skit.

16. Design a pirate game

You Wouldn't Want to Be a Pirate's Prisoner: Horrible Things You'd Rather Not Know, Malam

Create your own Old Pirate card game. Take a deck of cards and glue on pairs of pirate photos or drawings. Mark one card as Old Pirate. Use the same rules to play Old Pirate as you would for Old Maid. Copy figure 4.38 *Old Pirate Card Template* (see page 163), as many times as you need to cut and glue on a deck of cards.

17. Continue the adventure of Sindbad the sailor

Sindbad: From the Tales of the Thousand and One Nights, Zeman

After reading about the adventures of Sindbad the sailor, direct students to write and illustrate their own voyages of Sindbad, taking place on the route to China. Like the story in the book, they may create adventures using fantasy characters based on actual animals found in the ocean. Have students study patterns found in Persian carpets to create borders in their illustrations.

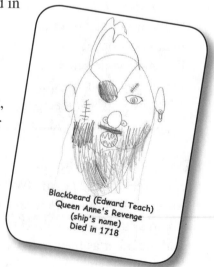

Blackbeard (Edward Teach)
Queen Anne's Revenge
(ship's name)
Died in 1718

18. Make pirate trading cards

The World of the Pirate, Garwood

Using the *Who's Who* section in the back of the book, and other reference sources, have students make their own pirate trading cards from cardstock or index cards. On each card, they should list information and draw a picture of that pirate. Students may trade completed cards with others.

19. Compare story elements

Robin Hook, Pirate Hunter!, Kimmel

Challenge students to compare story elements of *Robin Hook, Pirate Hunter* with that of a traditional tale of *Robin Hood*. How are they alike? Different?

20. List supplies needed for a pirate adventure

Imagine You're a Pirate, Clibbon
Pirate Pete Sets Sail, Jaggi

Ask students to list supplies they would need to pack for a pirate adventure on the high seas. Use the *Treasure Chest Worksheet* template figure 4.40 on page 164.

21. Learn to deal with the death of a pet

Tough Boris, Fox

Discuss why Tough Boris was sad. Ask children if they have ever had a pet that died, and what were some things that helped them feel better? Discuss how talking about fond memories of a pet could help them deal with grief. Read *The Tenth Good Thing About Barney*, by Judith Viorst, and brainstorm ten favorite memories Tough Boris might have had about his parrot.

22. Showcase collections

On the Go with Pirate Pete and Pirate Joe, Cannon

Pair up students and have them discuss personal collections. Have students sign up to share one of their collections with the class, and tell why they started their collection.

23. Create a Pirate Points fact book

See-Through Pirates, Davis

Instruct students to create a *Pirate Points* fact book on parchment paper or brown paper bags. List chores for all types of pirates on an entry page. Discuss with students how these chores compare to chores around the house.

24. Write about your own treasure

How I Became a Pirate, Long

Ask students to write about something they treasure. Is it something real or something from the heart, such as a friendship? Could you bury it? If so, where would you bury it and why?

Math

25. Write your own story problem

Mystery History of a Pirate Galleon, Finney

As a group, write a math story problem that includes adding or subtracting escudos, réals, doubloons, or pieces of eight. Refer to the chart on page 5 in Finney's book to calculate the equivalents. Have students write one of their own problems to give to another student to solve.

26. Graph a treasure map

Mystery History of a Pirate Galleon, Finney

Using a spreadsheet or graph paper, have students make a treasure map, similar to the one pictured in this book. Draw or insert clipart of islands, treasure chests, and pirate ships. Using their maps, have students challenge a partner to a Battleship™ game, utilizing the coordinates on their spreadsheet or graphing paper map.

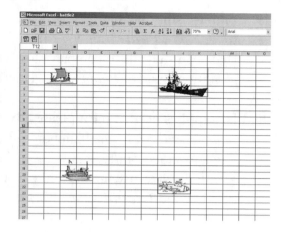

27. Navigate the high seas

Pirate, Platt

A Pirate's Life for Me: A Day Aboard a Pirate's Ship, Thompson

The World of the Pirate, Garwood

Have students research instruments used to navigate the seas including the cross-staff, the quadrant, and the compass. How did seamen use these tools to find their way? Students may learn more about the compass, and how it is used at <http://www.learn-orienteering.org/old/lesson1.html>

Science

28. Investigate bubbles

Edward and the Pirates, McPhail

Peggony-Po: A Whale of a Tale, Pinkney

Look at the bubbles depicted in *Edward and the Pirates* or in the ocean scene of *Peggony-Po*. Bubble makers can be made from a variety of materials, including a wire coat hanger. Bubble solution is made by adding a small amount of glycerin to equal parts water and dish detergent. Have children experiment with bubbles by dipping a variety of bubble wands in the solution. Does the shape or size of the wand determine the shape or size on the bubble? Use the Internet to investigate bubbles.

29. Describe historical treasure finds and retrievals

Sunken Treasure, Gibbons

True-Life Treasure Hunts, Donnelly

Use the format in the back of *Sunken Treasure* to create a form for students to use in describing other historical pirate finds. Include information about sinking, search and find, the salvage, restoration and preservation, and how this teaches about the past.

30. Recognize and define ship parts

Roger the Jolly Pirate, Helquist

Have one group of students use a hard copy dictionary and another group use an online dictionary to find the meaning of starboard, larboard, windward, leeward, mizzen, and main. Once they have finished, talk about the meaning of each ship part. Follow up with a discussion of strategies students used to find words quickly. Decide which method was most effective and why?

31. Understand the concept of floating and sinking

Pirate Pete Sets Sail, Jaggi

Use Styrofoam and miscellaneous items found around the room to construct model pirate ships. Have students predict which models will be most seaworthy. Sail models in a pool of water to determine which floated and which sank. What caused some to float and others to sink?

32. Investigate how history has changed navigation

Pirate, Lock

How has technology changed navigation? Have students use the following Web sites to research the history of navigation: Early Navigation Theme Page <www.cln.org/themes/early_navigation.html> or The History of Navigation – Boat Safe Kids! <www.boatsafe.com/kids/navigation.htm>. Compare the changes from compass and cross-staff to GPS (Global Positioning Systems) and satellites.

33. Investigate diseases pirates encountered

Pirates, Nickles

You Wouldn't Want to Be a Pirate's Prisoner, Malam

Diseases were often fatal to pirates. Have students investigate some of the illnesses or diseases pirates had to deal with, such as scurvy. They should include in their research whether the disease is still a problem today and note some of the cures. Have students log their findings in a journal or pirate's log. Additional help may be found at Wikipedia at <http://en.wikipedia.org/wiki/Scurvy>

34. Research and draw marine life

Pirate Pink and Treasures of the Reef, Day

Ask students to research the life cycle of one of the species of marine life that Pink encountered in the reef, and then draw a picture of it. Selections should be made from the book's end pages. Discuss how the end pages serve as an extension of the story.

Social Studies

35. Determine latitude and longitude

A Pirate's Life for Me: A Day Aboard a Pirate's Ship, Thompson

Sea Clocks: The Story of Longitude, Borden

Have students determine latitude and longitude. Investigate these Web sites: Social Studies for Kids <www.socialstudiesforkids.com/articles/geography/latitudelongitude.htm>. To locate the city in which they live, have students visit Latitude & Longitude - Look Up at <www.bcca.org/misc/qiblih/latlong_us.html>.

36. Explore the world of pirates

See-Through Pirates, Davis

Students learn to talk, dress, and act like a pirate at the following Web site: International Talk Like a Pirate Day <www.talklikeapirate.com/links.html#piratename>. List features common to the world of pirates.

37. Create a pirate handbook or slideshow presentation

The Pirate's Handbook: How to Become a Rogue of the High Seas, Lincoln

Create a pirate handbook. Divide the book into clothing, provisions, entertainment, conduct, charts and maps, ships, flags, attacks, treasure, punishment, pirate language, and pirate types. Pair each student with a partner to create each section. As an extension, students could compile a slideshow presentation.

38. Draw up a mock pirate resume

Pirates, Steele

A Pirates Life for Me, Thompson

The World of the Pirate, Garwood

Investigate pirate jobs and have students imagine they are applying for the position of pirate. What skills would they need? Have students write or type up a mock resume listing their skills.

39. Document a family heirloom

The Scrimshaw Ring, Jaspersohn

Discuss the meaning of an heirloom. After interviewing parents or grandparents to discover the story behind a family heirloom, have each student write a story about the heirloom and draw a picture of it. Share stories with the class and compile them in an heirloom book.

40. Analyze ship rules of conduct

The World of the Pirate, Garwood

What were some of the ships' rules of conduct and punishments pirates received for breaking them? Were the punishments fair? Have students discuss some of the rules of conduct in their school or library? Why is it necessary to have rules and regulations? Discuss the natural consequences of breaking these rules.

41. Make a wanted poster

Everything I Know About Pirates, Lichtenheld

Invite students to make a wanted poster and label it with their official pirate name. Students may refer to the chart in the book or go to <www.stupidstuff.org/main/piratename.htm>. At the Stupid Stuff Web site, each student enters his or her first and last name into this pirate name generator.

42. List the seven seas

Pirate, Lock

Pirates, Steele

Many pirate books refer to the seven seas. To list the seven seas, refer to the map in *Pirates* by Philip Steele or the "What are the seven seas?" Web site at <www.whoi.edu/info/seven-seas.html>. What are the four main oceans today? Challenge students to name the seven continents.

43. Create a notorious pirates timeline

Pirate Diary: The Journal of Jake Carpenter, Platt

Pirates, Steele

Develop a timeline of pirates. Include a time period and a description for each kind of pirate. Match each type of pirate to the type of ship they would have used.

44. Discuss values

The Sea Chest, Buzzeo

Talk about how finding a child in a sea chest changed Maita's life on the island. Ask students to think about what they value. Discuss why finding an infant in a sea chest would be more meaningful than any other type of treasure.

45. Research the life of a woman pirate

The Best Book of Pirates, Howard

Research the life of a woman pirate. Have students present their findings to the class. Look for information in the book or at the Women & the Sea: The Mariner's Museum Web site: <www.mariner.org/women/goingtosea/pirates.htm>.

46. Draw a map depicting the Pirate Round voyage

The Best Book of Pirates, Howard

Looking at the map on pages 6-7, create a map showing the voyage called the *Pirate Round*. Display a world map. Label the stops along the route. Include ports and the kinds of goods that could be found at each port, such as spices and silk.

47. Trace the Erie Canal Route

The Erie Canal Pirates, Kimmel

Trace the Erie Canal route using books or the Internet. Compare *The Erie Canal Pirates* book route to the actual route of the Erie Canal. Are they the same? See <www.eriecanal.org>. After reading the author's note, have students look at a map to see if they can get from Fairport to Lake Ontario without going on land. Find out if it would be possible to go up Niagara Falls.

48. Draw a map of an imaginary island

Pirate Pete, Kennedy

Pirates: Robbers of the High Seas, Gibbons

Have students draw a map of an imaginary island such as the fanciful Candy Island that Pirate Pete visited. Add lakes, rivers, mountains, and forests. Include a map key. Mark the spot where a treasure is buried. Describe the treasure and tell why it is important.

49. Design your own pirate trivia game

100 Things You Should Know About Pirates, Langley

Use pirate trivia located throughout the book to create a group trivia game. Students could create a computer slideshow of questions for others to answer.

50. Tie a knot

Pirates, Steele

After studying the bowline, the sheet bend, and the reef knot, give each student a length of rope and have them practice tying a variety of knots. Have students name a job for which each of these knots was best suited.

51. Call a playground truce

The Old Pirate of Central Park, Priest

A playground truce involves discussion, negotiation, and compromise. Write a truce for a potential playground situation. Have students role-play the incident, incorporating cards that are labeled, *Discuss, Negotiate,* and *Compromise* as the situation is moved to a resolution. Discuss why truces are necessary to achieve peace. As an extension of this activity, ask students to apply the concept to attempts to achieve world peace in today's world.

Art Arena

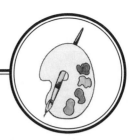

Winslow Homer

Winslow Homer was an American artist born in 1836. He grew up close to the ocean in Massachusetts, England, and Maine. In 1873, he painted, in oil, a picture of four young boys sailing with another much larger sailboat closer to the horizon. This picture is instrumental in teaching about perspective and the horizon line. Painting in the style of Winslow Homer reminds us of happy times on a beach. Help students complete their own paintings by drawing a horizon line on paper. Each student should use pencil to draw shells, fish, boats, and swimmers. Next, students paint with bright watercolors. After it dries, have students outline their drawings, adding detail with a black permanent marker.

Have students look at *Pirates, Ships, and Sailors* for classical pictures of the ocean and the end pages of *Pirate Pink and Treasures of the Reef* for simple examples of marine life to include in a painting. Students can learn more about Homer by reading *Winslow Homer* by Mike Venezia.

Theme Cuisine

Salmagundi

Historical Note:

Salmagundi dates back to the 17th century. It was a conglomeration of whatever ingredients pirates had on hand such as turtle, pigeon, fish, chicken, pork, goat meat, and whatever fruits or vegetables they could find. They would also add hardboiled eggs, pickled vegetables, and spices.

Kid Friendly Salmagundi (Chicken Stew) (8 Servings)
Ingredients:

2 pounds cooked chicken
2 cups chicken broth
2 cups cut carrots
2 cups cut celery
2 cups cut onions
2 cups potatoes cubed
¼ tsp. salt
¼ tsp. pepper

Directions:
Add ingredients to a crock-pot and cook until vegetables are tender. Give a sample serving to each student. Serve with crackers. (hardtack)

Banana Ice Cream Boats
(8 Servings)

Ingredients:

4 large bananas (each large banana makes two servings)
8 cookie wafers
32 candy coated chocolate pieces (4 per serving)
Chocolate syrup
Vanilla ice cream

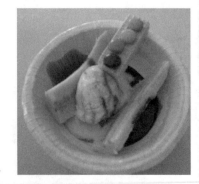

Directions:
Cut a banana in half, and then in half lengthwise. Place two sections in a bowl, as pictured. Place one scoop of ice cream in the center. Place the cookie wafer across to the edge of the bowl for the "plank." Use candy coated chocolate pieces for the pirates walking the plank. Use chocolate syrup for the water. Enjoy, Matey!

Culminating Activities

Transform the library or classroom into a maritime museum displaying paintings, ships, and other projects completed throughout the unit. Students serve as museum guides, leading other classes through the museum. Pirate books and pirate poetry may also be shared with guests. Share the book: *You Wouldn't Want to Be a Pirate's Prisoner.* After reviewing various jobs listed in this book, divide students into shipmate teams. Assign one person for each job, except for the seamen. Have each team follow clues in search of a hidden treasure. As teams arrive at destinations along the way, they will have to overcome an obstacle at each station before finding the clue to lead them to their next destination. As the teams progress, students discover how valuable it is to rely on one another to solve problems.

Sample problems for several destinations:
  a. Water supply is low. Stop to find fresh water. Measure the distance from your classroom to the water fountain.
  b. Captain gets sick and orders ship into port. Practice placing splints on each team member for three minutes.
  c. Sail rips in wind. Sit two minutes. Sew a five-inch seam on two pieces of fabric.
  d. Navigator plots wrong course. Sit two minutes and do 10 math problems before moving on to the next destination.
  e. Many of the crewmembers get scurvy. Everyone on the crew must eat an orange, lemon, or grapefruit slice.
  f. The ship bottoms out on a coral reef. Each member of the crew must draw a picture of a fish that could be found in the reef.
  g. The ship has sailed into a hurricane. Fill a sink with water. Unplug the sink and watch the funnel form as the water drains, to discover which way the water swirls before entering the drain. Do it twice to see if it goes the same way both times.

For more destinations, add a problem for each destination for which the crew can work out a solution. When both crews

arrive at their final destination, celebrate by serving Salmagundi and Banana Boats, singing pirate songs, and playing pirate games created during the unit.

Pirate Assessment Rubric

Students will be able to:	Fair 1	Good 2	Mastered 3	Score
Name 2 famous pirates				
Identify the parts of a ship and the types of ships used by pirates				
Understand mapping skills: latitude, longitude, legend, key, and direction				
List some weapons used by pirates				
Explain a Jolly Roger and why they had different designs				
Elaborate on consequences and punishments that took place onboard the ship				
Summarize the meaning of mutiny and treason				
Recall some of the jobs pirates had onboard their ships				
Share examples of modern day piracy and examine punishments				
Compile a list of jobs on a pirate ship and recall their importance				
Compare the clothing worn by different ranks of pirates				

Multimedia Resources

Captain Bogg & Salty: Pegleg Tango [sound recording] produced by Hendrickson/Hoskins LLC, 2005.

> Billed as "Piratical pop & buccaneer rock for scallywaggs of all ages," this CD contains a variety of upbeat songs and musical performances including topics of buccaneers, anchors, pieces of eight, life on a ship, and the pegleg tango (Grades 1-4).

Captain Jon's Island Adventure [video recording] directed by Jon and George C. Schellenger, 2004. 35 min.

    Captain Jon takes viewers on an adventure to a Caribbean island, Little Cayman, where students on a submarine ride explore life in the ocean depths, and learn ways to protect the ocean and its inhabitants (Grades K-3).

Sunken Treasure [video recording] produced by Reading Rainbow: GPN/WNED-TV, 1992. 30 min.

    LeVar Burton takes viewers on a treasure hunt to Pirates Cove in California, after looking at an old treasure map. Inspired by Gail Gibbons's book, *Sunken Treasure*, he uses a variety of methods to locate the treasure. Children are introduced to Dr. Robert Ballard, notorious for using science and technology to locate and explore the Titanic (Grades 2-5).

Web Site Resources

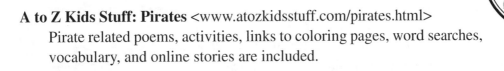

A to Z Kids Stuff: Pirates <www.atozkidsstuff.com/pirates.html>
    Pirate related poems, activities, links to coloring pages, word searches, vocabulary, and online stories are included.

Annie Silverjinks's Pirate Kingdom <http://pirateannie.fateback.com/>
    Pirate Annie hosts students on a pirate adventure that includes pirate tales, activities, graphics, and online adventure stories.

Expedition Whydah <www.whydah.com>
    Learn about the discovery and expedition of the cargo ship, Whydah, which was wrecked in a storm off Cape Cod on April 26, 1717. Read about artifacts that were recovered.

National Geographic Kids: Pirates <www.nationalgeographic.com/pirates>
    Uncover the secret booty by looking for clues in the pirate's log as you learn interesting facts about pirates. Included is an extensive biography of Blackbeard.

The New England Pirate Museum <www.piratemuseum.com/pirate.html>
    Pirate photos and educational materials that may be downloaded are available at this site, created by the New England Pirate Museum.

"Pirate"ly Speaking <www.leesummit.k12.mo.us/gifted/sgarland/..%5Cgiftedlsr7%5C pirates%5Cpirateweb.htm>
    Take up anchor and follow the links at this site to choose your own pirate adventure, take a pirate quiz, or perhaps take a virtual tour of a pirate museum.

Pirates! Fact & Legend <www.piratesinfo.com/main.php>
    This site has a lot of information on the history of pirates, biographies of famous pirates, pirate ships, codes of conduct, and Jolly Rogers.

Fiction Books

The Angel and Soldier Boy

by Peter Collington. Alfred A. Knopf, 1987.

After hearing a pirate bedtime story, a young child dreams that pirates break into her piggy bank and steal a coin. Through the heroic efforts of her toy angel and toy soldier, the treasure is recovered. Pastel illustrations evoke a gentle mood in this wordless adventure (Grades K-2).

Captain Abdul's Pirate School

by Colin McNaughton. Candlewick Press, 1994.

Sent to pirate school to toughen her up, Captain Maisy Pickles plans a school mutiny against the pirate teachers (Grades 2-4).

Do Pirates Take Baths?

by Kathy Tucker. Illus. Nadine Bernard Westcott. Albert Whitman & Company, 1994.

"How do you get to be a pirate?" "Where do pirates sleep?" These are just two of the questions posed about the life of pirates that are answered in rollicking rhyme (Grades K-2).

Edward and the Pirates

by David McPhail. Little, Brown and Company, 1997.

Edward is awakened by pirates who have come for his library book, to lead them to a buried treasure. When his parents order the pirates to stand in the corner, Edward hands over the book. Realizing they can't read, he reads aloud to them, as his parents return to bed (Grades K-2).

The Erie Canal Pirates

by Eric A. Kimmel. Illus. Andrew Glass. Holiday House, 2002.

Inspired by a folk song about the Erie Canal, Kimmel weaves a tale about an encounter between Captain Flynn and his men and Bill McGrew and his Erie Canal pirate crew. This lively tale ends with Flynn and crew sailing up Niagara Falls (Grades 2-4).

Everything I Know About Pirates: A Collection of Made-Up Facts, Educated Guesses, and Silly Pictures About Bad Guys of the High Seas
by Tom Lichtenheld. Simon & Schuster Books for Young Readers, 2000.
Humorous illustrations, paired with tongue-in-cheek answers, steal the show in this book of silly answers to questions about pirates (Grades K-3).

Henry & the Buccaneer Bunnies
by Carolyn Crimi. Illus. John Manders. Candlewick Press, 2005.
Captain Barnacle Black Ear's son, Henry, would rather read books than order prisoners to walk the plank. When a big storm approaches and Henry tries to warn the crew, no one takes him seriously until the storm arrives, and Henry uses book knowledge to save the day (Grades K-2).

How I Became a Pirate
by Melinda Long. Illus. David Shannon. Harcourt, Inc., 2003.
When Jeremy Jacob is invited to join a pirate crew, he is happy to be aboard, until he realizes that pirates don't tuck one in, read a bedtime story, or give a goodnight kiss (Grades K-2).

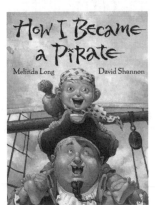

I Spy Treasure Hunt: A Book of Picture Riddles
by Jean Marzollo. Photos by Walter Wick. Scholastic Inc., 1999.
Through a story told in rhyming verses, readers are asked to locate objects hidden in the photographs and to solve the riddles. Photographs depict Smuggler's Cove, items from a treasure chest, a map, a lighthouse, an island, and more (Grades K-2).

Imagine You're a Pirate
by Meg Clibbon. Illus. Lucy Clibbon. Annick Press: Firefly Books Ltd., 2001.
This humorous look at present day children becoming pirates includes a pirate code, pirate clothing, the Jolly Roger, famous pirates, and pirate food (Grades K-3).

It Was a Dark and Stormy Night
by Janet and Allan Ahlberg. Penguin Group: Viking, 1993.
On a dark and stormy night, the chief of the brigands, who had kidnapped Antonio, said to him, "I'm bored-tell us a story!" Thus begins the story spun by an eight-year-old that draws in pirates, cannons, and the smell of hot chocolate, upon return from what his parents term "A likely adventure" (Grades 2-4).

Maggie and the Pirate

by Ezra Jack Keats. Four Winds Press, 1979, 1987.
When Maggie's pet cricket comes up missing, she discovers a new kid dressed as a pirate in a tree house holding Nikki's cage. A scuffle ensues and the cricket is accidentally killed. Maggie returns home and the new kid comes over with an explanation and another cricket. The story ends with two new friends listening to the wonderful sound of crickets (Grades K-2).

Molly Limbo

by Margaret Hodges. Illus. Elizabeth Miles. Atheneum Books for Young Readers, 1996.
In this story inspired by an old English folktale, Mr. Means purchases a haunted house by the sea and hires someone to cook and clean, until he discovers that the ghost of Molly Limbo is doing part of the work. When he fires the widow, the ghost rebels by leaving the house a mess. Miserly Mr. Means reemploys Mrs. Handy, who returns but declines his marriage proposal (Grades 2-4).

The Old Pirate of Central Park

by Robert Priest. Houghton Mifflin Company, 1999.
A retired pirate and a retired queen meet up in Central Park while sailing their replica ships in the pond. A battle ensues over who will rule the waters, until the queen calls a truce, realizing that she is late for her noon nap. The story ends with a newly formed friendship (Grades K-2).

On the Go with Pirate Pete and Pirate Joe

by A.E. Cannon. Illus. Elwood H. Smith. Penguin Group: Viking, 2002.
Pirate Pete and Pirate Joe share likes, dislikes, and personal collections, as they attempt to become true pirates by looking for a ship and a parrot in this easy reading story (Grades K-2).

Peggony-Po: A Whale of a Tale

by Andrea Davis Pinkney. Illus. Brian Pinkney. Hyperion Books for Children: Jump at the Sun, 2006.
In this original tall tale, a sailor boy carved from driftwood comes to life and vows to seek revenge on Cetus, the monstrous whale responsible for biting off his father's leg. Pinkney's striking scratchboard illustrations bring the sumptuous adventure to life (Grades 1-4).

The Pigrates Clean Up

by Steven Kroll. Illus. Jeni Bassett. Henry Holt and Company, Inc., 1993.
As the pigrates prepare for their captain's wedding, a flurry of activity ensues aboard the ship, from swabbing the deck to taking a bath, described in rhyming verses (Grades K-2).

Pirate Diary: The Journal of Jake Carpenter

by Richard Platt. Illus. Chris Riddell. Candlewick Press, 2001.
The year is 1716 and nine-year-old Jake Carpenter is about to

join his Uncle Will and become a sailor on the Sally Anne. He ends up becoming a pirate, encounters a sea monster, and spies on a mermaid (Grades K-6).

Pirate Pete

by Kim Kennedy. Illus. Doug Kennedy. Harry N. Abrams, Inc., 2002.
Learning that the queen has discovered a treasure map, Pirate Pete and his parrot go off in search of the gold, eventually ending up at Mermaid's Island. There, the queen thwarts their plan, leaving them marooned. Discovering their boat, it is off into the sunset in search of more gold (Grades K-2).

Pirate Pete Sets Sail

by Jean-Pierre Jaggi. Trans. J. Alison James. Illus. Alan Clarke. North-South Books, 2003.
Pirate Pete sets sail for a new island with his parrot and mates in tow, only the journey is actually a move to a new home and the mates are his parents. Docking at the new house, Pete explores its contents, creating a fanciful adventure for himself (Grades K-2).

Pirate Pink and Treasures of the Reef

by Jan Day. Illus. Janeen I. Mason. Pelican Publishing Company, 2003.
Redbeard's daughter prefers to explore the high seas than have tea with her mother. Pirate Pink's daytime adventure with a friend takes her to Turtle Bay, where they find jewels in an abandoned ship and discover marine life. When pirates return, with the help of a shark and sea turtle, the friends flee. It becomes clear that the real treasure in the bay is marine life (Grades K-2).

Pirate Treasure

by Loretta Krupinski. Penguin Young Readers Group: Dutton Children's Books. 2006.
Captain Oliver and his first mate have difficulty making friends. After settling in a small village, a storm comes up and their sailing expertise and ability to predict the weather saves the village. Friendship with the villagers of Mousam is declared the greatest treasure of all (Grades K-3).

Pirateology: The Pirate Hunter's Companion

edited by Dugald A. Steer. Illus. Ian Andrew, Anne Yvonne Gilbert, Helen Ward, et al. Candlewick Press, 2006.
Based on the sea journal of Captain William Lubber, and the contents of an 18th century sea chest, Lubber and his crew of 80 sailors set out to capture Arabella Drummond, terror of the seas, and recover the stolen treasure, in this engaging paper engineered book (Grades 1-5).

Robin Hook, Pirate Hunter!

by Eric A. Kimmel. Illus. Michael Dooling. Scholastic Press, 2001.

When notorious Captain James Hook finds a young boy being rocked in the arms of an octopus, he decides to raise him as his own. When he discovers that Robin doesn't like to make prisoners walk the plank and, in fact, helps them escape, Hook leaves him on an island. Robin befriends the island creatures and is selected by the lost boys to become their captain. Thus begins the legend of Robin Hook who foils pirate plans and rescues the helpless (Grades 1-3).

Roger the Jolly Pirate

by Brett Helquist. HarperCollins Publishers, 2004.

Jolly Roger's lack of pirate sense makes him the target of ridicule among his shipmates until his accidental concoction, an exploding cake, is instrumental in winning a battle (Grades 2-4).

The Scrimshaw Ring

by William Jaspersohn. Illus. Vernon Thornblad. The Vermont Folklife Center, 2002.

Based on real events that occurred in Newport, Rhode Island around 1710, a young boy known for weaving fanciful tales, tells the story of a band of mutineers who embark on his home while his parents are out. After burying the captain and the first mate, a mutineer who sees the boy cowering in a corner, gives him his ring. When the boy's parents return, the scrimshaw ring and gravesites are proof that his story really did happen (Grades 2-3).

The Sea Chest

by Toni Buzzeo. Illus. Mary GrandPre. Dial Books for Young Readers, 2002.

Auntie Maita shares with her great grandniece the legend of a treasure chest that washed ashore one stormy night, containing a baby. Seaborne is raised as Auntie Maita's sister and the circle continues, as the little girl hearing the story awaits her parents' return from across the Atlantic, where they have traveled to fetch a tiny stranger who will become her new sister (Grades K-3).

Shiver Me Letters: A Pirate ABC

by June Sobel. Illus. Henry Cole. Harcourt, Inc., 2006.

When the Captain states that *R* is not enough to keep his pirates tough, the crew sets out to capture the other letters of the alphabet. Letters show up in unique places, depicted in comical drawings, as the crew proceeds to plunder every letter of the alphabet (Grades K-2).

Sindbad: From the Tales of the Thousand and One Nights

retold by Ludmila Zeman. Tundra Books, 1999.

Shahrazad devises a plan to enthrall an evil king with stories for one thousand and one nights. The adventures of a sailor named Sindbad include tales of a paradise that turns out to be the back of a whale and the discovery of a valley filled with diamonds (Grades 2-6).

To Capture the Wind

by Sheila MacGill-Callahan. Illus. Gregory Manchess. Dial Books for Young Readers, 1997.

There are four riddles Oonagh, an Irish maiden, must answer in order to unite Princess Ethne with her lover and escape from the pirate king Malcolm. Oonagh frees her lover, solves the riddles, and unites the princess Ethne with her lover, Aiden. In response to how to capture the wind on water, Oonagh invents sails. Oil paintings depict the Celtic world (Grades 2-6).

Tough Boris

by Mem Fox. Illus. Kathryn Brown. Harcourt Brace & Company, 1994.

Boris von der Borch is scruffy, greedy, and fearless, like other pirates, until his parrot dies and he cries and cries, demonstrating that even the toughest of pirates has compassion (Grades K-2).

Anthology Books

The Barefoot Book of Pirates

retold by Richard Walker. Illus. Olwyn Whelan. Barefoot Books, 1998.

Pirate tales from around the world make up this seafaring collection. Charming illustrations complement the anthology inspired by legends and historical records from Scandinavia, England, Germany, Ireland, Japan, Scotland, and Morocco (Grades 2-6).

The Book of Pirates

selected by Michael Hague. HarperCollins Publishers, 2001.

Traditional tales and poems about pirates, by the likes of Robert Louis Stevenson, Arthur Conan Doyle, and Washington Irvin, captivate intermediate readers (Grades 3-6).

The Pirate Princess: And Other Fairy Tales

by Neil Philip. Illus. Mark Weber. Scholastic Inc.: Arthur A. Levine Books, 2005.

In the first tale of this anthology, a princess becomes a pirate in a quest to find her true love. Along the way, she encounters a king who showers her with gifts and a merchant's son who views her as a prize. Eventually, she is reunited with her true love, the prince (Grades 3-6).

Pirates, Ships, and Sailors

by Kathryn and Byron Jackson. Illus. Gustaf Tenggren. Random House: A Golden Book, 1950/2006.

This charmingly illustrated collection of stories and poems, first issued in 1950, includes stories about a pirate's cove, a ship in a bottle, the flying Dutchman, and more (Grades K-3).

Information Books

100 Things You Should Know About Pirates

by Andrew Langley. Miles Kelly Publishing, LTD, 2006.

Did you know that the original buccaneers were drifters or criminals on the island of Hispaniola who hunted wild pigs for supper? Little known facts about the world of pirates are included in this book (Grades 2-6).

The Best Book of Pirates

by Barnaby Howard. Illus. Angus McBride et al. Kingfisher Publications, 2002.

What were pirates really like? Readers are taken on an adventure of the high seas to learn about life on board a pirate ship, pirate travel routes, and notorious pirates (Grades 2-6).

Blackbeard: Eighteenth-Century Pirate of the Spanish Main and Carolina Coast

by Aileen Weintraub. The Rosen Publishing Group, Inc., PowerKids Press, 2002.

Blackbeard's life, death, and legends are covered, including stories about how, as one of the most feared pirates of all time, he instilled fear in others (Grades K-4).

How to Be a Pirate

by John Malam. Illus. Dave Antram. National Geographic Society, 2005.

In the 1700's, travel to the New World is filled with dangerous people but safe for those who live outside the law. Readers learn to navigate, recognize Jolly Rogers, and steal booty from enemy ships in this handbook on becoming a pirate (Grades 1-4).

Mystery History of a Pirate Galleon

by Fred Finney. Illus. Mike Bell, Richard Berridge, and Roger Hutchins. The Millbrook Press: Copper Beech Books, 1996.

Mystery sleuths feel like they are living in a pirate galleon as they are challenged to discover the whereabouts of a treasure-stealing pirate through clues, puzzles, and brain teasers (Grades 2-4).

Pirate

by Deborah Lock. Illus. Peter Bull. DK Publishing, Inc., 2005.

Readers learn about pirates, privateers, The Jolly Roger, and other pirate fare (Grades K-2).

Pirate

by Richard Platt. Photos by Tina Chambers. DK Publishing, Inc., 1994, 2004.

This Eyewitness book educates the reader in all aspects of pirate life and lore, spanning women pirates to pirates found in literature, film, and theater (Grades 3-6).

The Pirate Queen

by Emily Arnold McCully. G.P. Putnam's Sons, 1996.

Tales of the Irish woman pirate include a meeting with Queen Elizabeth of England who grants her maintenance from Sir Richard Bingham's lands and accepts her offer to defend the Crown (Grades 3-6).

Pirates

by Greg Nickles and Bobbie Kalman. Crabtree Publishing Company, 1997.

Crafts and games are included in this title detailing the lifestyle of 1600 and 1700 pirates, covering topics of ships and pirate crew to clothing and sea life (Grades 1-4).

Pirates

by Philip Steele. Consultant: David Cordingly. Lorenz Books, 1999.

Young artists explore the world of pirates through 16 illustrated projects. Becoming a pirate, charting waters, and going on coastal raids is a sampling of themes (Grades 3-6).

A Pirate's Life for Me! A Day Aboard a Pirate Ship

by Julie Thompson and Brownie Macintosh. Illus. Patrick O'Brien. Charlesbridge Publishing, 1996.

A day aboard a pirate ship is brought to life as the scenario begins with all hands on deck patching sails, climbing ratlines, and hoisting The Jolly Roger (Grades 2-4).

Pirates! Raiders of the High Seas

by Christopher Maynard. DK Publishing, Inc., 1998.

This fictional first person account of piracy and notorious pirates offers a glimpse at what life was like for these raiders of the high seas (Grades 2-4).

Pirates: Robbers of the High Seas

by Gail Gibbons. Little, Brown and Company, 1993.
Based on true accounts of legendary pirates and their ships, Gibbons captures the danger and drama of the battles ensued between robbers of the high seas and honest sailors (Grades K-2).

Sea Clocks: The Story of Longitude

by Louise Borden. Illus. Erik Blegvad. Simon & Schuster: Margaret K. McElderry Books, 2004.
In the days in which sailors could measure latitude, but not longitude, John Harrison's sea clock solved those problems. The Royal Observatory became the location of the prime meridian. The world set its clocks according to Greenwich Mean Time (Grades 2-6).

See-Through Pirates

by Kelly Davis. Running Press Book Publishers: Running Press Kids, 2003.
Filled with historical facts and biographies of notorious pirates, this comprehensive book includes colorful see-through plates that afford readers a special way of looking at pirate ships, weapons, looted treasures, and pirate attacks (Grades 2-4).

Sunken Treasure

by Gail Gibbons. Thomas Y. Crowell, 1988.
Gibbons illustrates current techniques used to locate and retrieve sunken treasure. The search for treasure buried in a Spanish galleon in 1622 is detailed, followed by a description of the sinking, find, salvage, and modern day conclusions about several other sunken ships (Grades K-2).

True-Life Treasure Hunts

by Judy Donnelly. Illus. Thomas La Padula. Random House, 1984, 1993.
This high-interest *Step-Into-Reading* book describes true-life treasure hunts, beginning with a treasure buried by an earthquake in Jamaica in 1692 (Grades 2-4).

The World of the Pirate

by Val Garwood. Illus. Richard Berridge. Peter Bedrick Books, 1997.
From early sea robbers to pirates, buccaneers, and modern day pirates in the South China seas, the world of pirates is explored (Grades 3-6).

You Wouldn't Want to Be a Pirate's Prisoner: Horrible Things You'd Rather Not Know

by John Malam. Illus. David Antram. Created and designed by David Salariya. Franklin Watts, 2002.
Consequences of being a pirate's prisoner are detailed, that often included a flogging or being marooned on a deserted island (Grades 2-6).

Activity Books

The Great Pirate Activity Book
by Deri Robins. Illus. George Buchanan. Kingfisher, 1995.
This pirate activity book includes instructions for making a pirate kit, treasure-hunting game, treasure chest, and more. Also included is a hall of historical pirates (Grades K-3).

Kids Can Draw Pirates
by Philippe Legendre. Walter Foster Publishing, Inc. 2002.
In this beginning drawing book, pictures are created by combining geometric shapes to form a mass of volumes and surfaces. This first look at composition, proportion, shape, and lines, includes models for drawing a Jolly Roger, pirate ship, treasure chest and more (Grades 1-4).

Pirates
by Rachel Wright. Sea-to-Sea Publications, 2005.
Historical facts and related craft activities assist young explorers in areas such as pirate dress and duties, mapmaking, and knot tying. Biographical sketches of Blackbeard, Anne Bonny, Mary Read, and other notorious pirates are included (Grades 2-6).

The Pirate's Handbook: How to Become a Rogue of the High Seas
by Margarette Lincoln. Dutton: Cobblehill Books, 1995.
Facts about pirate life and customs, information about notorious pirates and treasure islands, and activities for a treasure map, pirate flag, and more are included in this handbook (Grades 2-4).

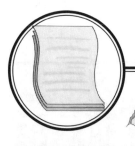

 Pirate Fairy Tales Elements Chart

Name of Fairy Tale	Special Words	Good Character	Evil Character	Royalty, Castle	Magic	Problem and Solution	Things in 3's or 7's

Figure 4.32 Pirate Fairy Tale Elements Chart

Name _____

Software Piracy Worksheet

Please go to http://www.uspto.gov/go/kids/
kidantipiracy.htm and answer the following questions.

What are three types of intellectual property?

_____

_____

_____

What is the definition of software piracy?

_____

What are two ways of knowing (indicators) that something is copyrighted?

_____

_____

What is intellectual property that is not protected by copyright restrictions called?

_____

How do you think software piracy hurts the owner of the intellectual property?

_____

_____

On a separate paper share your ideas about the following:

    What could you do to help stop piracy?
    What do you think the laws and punishments should be for pirating
      intellectual property?

Figure 4.33 Software Piracy Worksheet

Walk the Plank

By Steve Presser

"Walk the plank boy!" The captain yelled,
"You haven't been doing your chores!
You don't row below or swab the decks
Or help us win any wars!"

So I took four steps, got a big bounce,
And did three flips in the air,
Then two full twists into a swan dive
Just to add some flair.

I went in smoothly, the water was nice
And I floated right up with a smile,
Then swam away from the filthy boat
And treaded some water awhile.

A turtle named Myrtle chewed on the rope
That was keeping my two hands tied,
Then two friendly dolphins picked me up
And took me to an island nearby.

We swam all day, I didn't do chores,
Just ate coconuts in the sun,
And now the guys don't walk the plank
'Cause the Captain knows it's fun.

Figure 4.34 Walk the Plank

Old Pirate Card Template

Figure 4.38 Old Pirate Card Template

Treasure Chest Template

Figure 4.40 Treasure Chest Template

INDEX

Jousting 72

K

Kings 45, 71, 76, 78, 80, 110, 119

Knights 44, 45, 46, 57, 60, 62, 67, 69, 70, 74, 75, 76, 77, 78, 80, 81, 83

Knots 135, 144

L

Labyrinth 59

Lance 54–55

Lancelot 70–71, 77

Language arts 8, 12–14, 48, 56–59, 93, 97–99, 134, 137–139

Latitude 131, 132, 142, 158

Legends 26, 56, 67, 68, 69, 70, 71, 73, 74, 99, 112, 154

Longitude 131, 132, 142, 158

M

Magic Tree House
  Books 3, 43–44, 87–88, 129–130
  Activities 4–6, 44–46, 88–91, 130–132

Magnolia 5

Maps 5, 17, 18, 61, 89, 90, 102, 110, 130, 131, 140, 142, 143, 144

Marine life 141, 145, 153

Math 8, 14–15, 48, 59, 93, 99, 134, 139–140

Medieval
  Clothing 51, 52, 53, 55, 66, 67, 75
  Feast 44, 48, 56, 60
  Timeline 56

Merlin 51, 71

Middle Ages (See medieval)

Mirage 89

Monastery 56, 57

Moon 16, 23

Multimedia 21, 66, 73, 109, 148

Mummies 87, 88, 95, 97, 100, 104, 107, 109, 110, 113, 114, 121

Music 53, 57, 58, 66, 71, 97, 109, 136, 148

Mythology 60, 71, 97, 101, 113, 116

N

Navigation 141

Nefertari 99, 101, 113

P

Paleontology 22, 28, 30

Papier-Mache 9, 10, 90–91

Parrots 131

Passport 1, 41, 85, 127

Peasants 67, 81

Phoenix 103

Pieces of eight 139, 148

Pirates
  Notorious 132, 143, 156, 157, 158, 159
  Women 143, 159

Poetry 11, 59, 84, 96, 98, 120, 135, 137, 138

Princesses 53, 60, 70, 113, 155

Privateers 132, 157

Pteranodon 3, 4, 5, 31

Pterosaur 10, 25, 31

Pyramids 88, 89, 96, 97, 101, 103, 110, 115, 116, 118, 119

Q

Queens 78, 110, 113

R

Recipes 50, 100, 117
  Apple tarts 64
  Ataif pancakes 104
  Banana ice cream boats 146
  Dinosaur bones 20
  Dirt Dig pudding 19
  Gingerbread 64
  Mummy bread sticks 104
  Salmagundi 146

Robin Hood 51, 52, 67, 68, 69

Rules of chivalry 57

Rules of conduct 142

S

Saint George 73

Sarcophagus 95, 106

Science 15, 59, 99, 140

Scrimshaw 136, 142, 154

Seven seas 143

Shabtis 90

Shaduf 100

Shields 54, 101

Ships 130, 140, 141, 142, 146, 147, 156, 157, 158

Sinbad 138, 154

Social Studies 8, 16–18, 48, 60–62, 94, 100–102, 134, 142–144

Soil 8, 90

Songs (See music)

Sound recordings (See multimedia)

Stained Glass 48, 49, 50, 68, 81

Station rotations 9, 49, 94, 135

Symmetry 94, 99, 103, 106

T

Tall tales 14

Technology 9, 80, 135, 137, 149

Theme Cuisine 19, 64, 104, 146

Timeline 17, 56, 97, 143

Tournament 46, 74

Trade routes 61

Travel itinerary 2, 42, 86, 128

Treasure 139, 140, 149, 151, 153, 158, 164

Treasure Hunt 132, 149, 151

Trivia 15, 29, 52, 66, 144

Troubador 57

Tutankhamen 102, 103, 109, 110, 119, 120

Tutankhamun (See Tutankhamen)
Tyrannosaurus rex 21, 26

V

Van Gogh, Vincent 18–20
Videotapes (See multimedia)

W

Weapons 67, 77, 80, 117, 132
Weaving 52
Web
    Book 7, 47, 92, 133
    Curriculum 8, 48, 94, 134
Women 76, 79, 80, 117, 143, 157
Word wall 3, 43, 87, 129

Curriculum Connections for Tree House Travelers for Grades K-4